THE
NINETIES

THE NINETIES

Personal Recollections of the 20th Century

•

Gloria Wood and Paul Thompson

With photographs by
Grace Robertson

BBC BOOKS

To my mother —
a wonderful talker who at the age of eighty was too young
to be included in this book

GLORIA WOOD

●

ISBN 0 563 36943 4 (hardback)
ISBN 0 563 36785 7 (paperback)

First published by BBC Books,
a division of BBC Enterprises Limited
Woodlands, 80 Wood Lane, London W12 0TT

Set in 11/13 Janson by Selwood Systems, Midsomer Norton
Printed and bound in Great Britain by
Butler & Tanner Ltd, Frome, Somerset
Jacket printed by
Lawrence Allen Ltd, Weston-super-Mare

Contents

THE AUTHORS

Gloria Wood, having graduated from Newcastle University, worked in journalism, publishing and then television, mainly on documentaries where she specialised in social history programmes. She produced the film 'And They Sailed Away' for *The Nineties* series. She lives in Gloucestershire with her partner and four children.

Paul Thompson, who was consultant to *The Nineties* series, is Research Professor of Social History at the University of Essex and Director of the National Life Story Collection in London. Internationally known as a social and oral historian, he is founder-editor of *Oral History* and his books include *The Edwardians, The Voice of the Past* and *I Don't Feel Old.*

THE PHOTOGRAPHER

Grace Robertson began taking pictures professionally while still in her teens. Self-taught, her lyrical and warmly humorous images appeared mainly in the illustrated magazine *Picture Post.* A monograph of her distinctive photojournalism was published in 1989, and she was the subject of a Channel 4 documentary. Her photographs are in the permanent collections of the Victoria and Albert Museum, London, the National Museum of Photography, Bradford, and in many private collections in Britain and America. In 1992 an exhibition of her work was held in Washington D.C. She was commissioned to photograph the contributors to *The Nineties* series and an exhibition of these photographs was held at the National Theatre, London, in 1993.

PICTURE CREDITS

The photographs on the following pages were taken by Grace Robertson: 18, 25, 26, 31, 32, 38, 47, 53, 56, 57, 59, 60, 62, 67, 73, 77, 79, 83, 88, 93, 97, 102, 106, 111, 116, 120, 123, 129, 135, 147, 152, 155, 159, 163, 169, 174 (above), 176, 181 (above), 186 (above), 190 (above).

We are very grateful to the contributors who kindly allowed us to use photographs from their own collections: 22, 28, 35, 40, 43, 48, 55, 58, 64, 65, 70, 74, 76, 80, 86, 90, 94, 98, 100, 104, 107, 108, 113, 114, 118, 121, 126, 131, 138, 140, 142, 154, 157, 160, 166, 170, 174 (below), 177, 181 (below), 186 (below), 188, 190 (below).

Additional photographs were supplied by: Gordon Elsbury 74; Keith Ellis 84; *The Daily Mirror* 96.

Preface

The idea of *The Nineties* was conceived by Peter Salmon, and Sam Organ was involved in its early development. Annie Paul was executive producer of the television series and Florence Minnis assistant producer; the programme producers were Jenny Abbott ('I Married a Stranger'), Kate Broome ('All Your Kisses Are Mine' and 'We Grinned and Beared It'), Clara Glynn ('The Demon in the Glass'), Pat Holland ('Fresh Air and Fun'), Annie Paul ('Life's a Gamble, Innit?'), Deborah Wignall ('Pennies on their Eyes') and Gloria Wood ('And They Sailed Away'). Paul Thompson was consultant to the series. Martin Kiszko composed the music. The research and production team also included Miriam Akhtar, Steven Clarke, Val Harvey, Tim Jordan, Joe Kennedy, Jennie Milner, Rabinder Minhas, Rai Patterson, Heather Petersen, Suzie Sampson, Annie Venables and Liz Wilson; the film crew Garry Morrison, Mike Thomas and Steve Williams; and the editors Mike Kleinsteuber, Andrew Findlay, Liz Thoyts, Ian Pitch and Peter Simpson.

The book has drawn on all their work, but especially the advice of Annie Paul and Florence Minnis, and the documentary photography of Grace Robertson. Gloria Wood's manuscript was typed by Kim Wilkins.

Above all, both the series and the book have depended on the very many ninety-year-olds who gave so much of their time, answered the questions of researchers and producers with such patience, and told such fascinating stories. In the end both the series and the book had the space for only a fraction of the memories which they recorded. The choice depended not just on the individual's story but equally on how it could contribute to a thematic programme or chapter. Not everybody who was shown on screen is in the book, and there are also some people who were filmed and kept in the book but not in the final programmes: basically because the two forms of communication are different. For the same reason the printed word demands active editing from the raw transcripts, but in this book the original words recorded are retained throughout, and editing is used only to bring out the speaker's meaning. Lastly, all the original recordings are being archived, whether or not they were used for the programmes or the book. For neither would have been possible without the full range of memories recorded, and these recordings will remain as a unique resource for historians and broadcasters in the future.

Introduction: On the Horizon

As time propels us all relentlessly towards the end of the twentieth century, so the memory of the first decades of our century is receding. Only a tiny band of First World War veterans now comes to the Cenotaph each November to celebrate the Armistice. Even the memory of the great slump and unemployment in the thirties has long ceased to swing elections. If you start chatting to an old person in a bus today about their memories of the past, you are unlikely to find yourself listening to stories that come from earlier than 1920. The First World War seems in the twilight of memory; the world before it, over the horizon.

The astonishing achievement of *The Nineties* is to show that we can still hear directly, from men and women who experienced those years, what it was like to live through the first decades of this century. And more than that, we can hear powerfully and clearly. That is the unique quality of 'oral history', history based on the memories of living survivors, in contrast to the silent old newspapers and boxes of archived documents from which most historians have to construct their accounts of the past. There are many ways in which a chasm separates us from the world at the turn of this century, a world in which Britain was the greatest nation, ruling a quarter of the globe directly, dominating the international economy with the products of its factories, and a maritime nation too, with the world's biggest shipping fleet. Yet it was also a Britain of desperate poverty, in which unskilled workers could not earn enough to eat, let alone to buy a newspaper; and in which the sexual and emotional expressiveness which younger people today take for granted was a distant dream of utopian radical reformers. You have to imagine a Britain in which a doctor working in a poor working-class neighbourhood knew that a third of all the babies born to its families would die within their first year; a Britain in which a father might have the absolute power to veto his daughter's suitors and cut off all contact with them; in which a young bride could recoil in astonished horror from the first sight of a naked male on her wedding night. *The Nineties* bridges that chasm, tells us what such experiences really felt like.

Just because the witnesses who speak in *The Nineties* are rare survivors, the making of the television programmes on which this book is based has been in a sense an unveiling process, the discovery of an almost invisible village scattered all around us, populated by people in their nineties or above, most of whom have too few chances to speak about themselves and their lives. As you read their stories, it is almost like rediscovering a lost community. Or perhaps like looking westwards from the cliffs of Cornwall after sunset, and catching a glimpse of the lights of the legendary lost land of Lyonesse over the horizon: except that the testimonies of *The Nineties* come across to us in full clarity.

Yet however remarkable its messages about the past, this book also conveys something very important about living in the present: about the vitality and resilience which seems one of the essential ingredients for successful survival into very old age. Twenty years ago, when I first used 'oral history' myself, interviewing for my book *The Edwardians*, I thought of the old people as sources almost like old newspapers or the other documents which social historians use: sources to be read simply for the topics and the time period which I wanted to know about. I even tried to cut short their memories at 1920. But very soon, along with others beginning to work with oral history at the same time, I found that interviewing was quite different from reading old documents. Success depends on a mutual human rapport and respect, above all on an ability to listen, to hear the unexpected; and a good interview can be emotionally powerful on both sides. Because many older people are much too rarely taken seriously, simply being listened to in an interview can give them a new spark of courage and sense of purpose.

One of the offshoots of oral history has been the group reminiscent work which is now widespread in hospitals and social centres. Historians on their side have increasingly shifted towards recording a whole life story which tells not only about earlier years but also what has happened since, and what life means today. The great variety of ways – some of them very creative – in which people find meaning in later life is indeed the theme of my own most recent book, *I Don't Feel Old*. And in their few months of work the rolling group of young researchers and producers led by Annie Paul who made up *The Nineties* team – involving altogether twelve women and three men – has undergone a similarly transforming experience. The result has been a television series and a book which are primarily shaped around whole lives: a past which leads through to now.

There are still living in Britain today some quarter of a million women and men who were born under Queen Victoria and grew up as young Edwardians. They have lived under six monarchs. Just a few of them can remember the Boer War; many of the men fought in the First World War and many of the women lost their men in it; and all of them lived on to hear the bombing of British cities in the Second World War. When they were small, men fought wars on horseback, but by the time they were middle-aged the Americans were killing tens of thousands with a single nuclear bomb on a Japanese city. They were middle-aged too when the British Empire, which had framed many of their lives, dissolved; and were already elderly when Britain entered Europe.

The political heroes of their youth were the last Liberal prime ministers, Asquith and Lloyd George, and of their early adulthood the Conservative Baldwin. They saw Churchill turn from a radical reforming Liberal to a defiant Conservative. They witnessed the tentative first Labour coalition governments in the 1920s and the great landslide victory of 1945 which heralded the setting up of the welfare state and the nationalisation of the economic infrastructure; and then when they were in their eighties, they watched it all dismantled in the name of the 'Victorian values' with which they had grown up. They saw the trade unions similarly rise from small minority societies, mainly of skilled craftsmen, to a position of immense national power, confronting government and employers in the turbulent years of the Edwardian 'Labour unrest' and the General Strike, working in partnership with government from the 1940s, and now again ousted.

They themselves mostly started work before the outbreak of the First World War, at a time when three-quarters of all in employment were manual workers, and coal miners the largest single group among them. They first married – if at all, because especially many of the women among them never found a partner – during the 1920s. The women who married almost all then gave up paid work, although a few took it up again later on, when their children were older and the hostility to married women as workers had begun to wane. The men, by contrast, were either in paid work, or in military service, right through until the 1960s, unless they suffered periods of unemployment, especially in the worst slump years of the early thirties.

Through their lives, in short, we have a snapshot of the social history of our century – and through most of it, we can imagine what they might have been experiencing. But surprisingly, the nearer we get to the present, the harder such guesses become. What has happened to them in their last thirty years? We certainly know from surveys how poverty increases with age, and also physical disability; but much less about what ordinary life is like beyond the age of ninety. So the television team were venturing into virgin territory. More than that, they were looking for a kind of person who is a bit special at any age: who can tell the story of their life compellingly. To find them, the invisible village had to be staked out and searched.

Altogether over six thousand potential contributors were found. Two-thirds of the initial contacts came in response to advertisements in the *Radio Times*, national and local newspapers, and to radio appeals; the remainder were traced through special searches, including help from those caring for the elderly. These first responses included letters which gave some intriguing hints of what might be in store. For example, David Taylor wrote:

I was bought 1898 am 93. I have seen many changes & happenings, being a native of Hulme Manchester saw the uproar when Mrs Pankhurst were on the March... As for Memories at 3 & 4 years old can remember the excitement of the Boer War & King Edward the Seventh & Queen Alexandra Coronation, 1901–2... At the age of 10–11 I got a job as a Lather Boy going after School 5 till 8 or Saturday 9 am till 12 pm, that's when men came in for their penny Shave. Me & the Barbers son were very busy lathering & we had to rub the Lather well in the Chin as most men only Shaved once a week. Scruffy hat, Barber worked like lightning... I have many other things we kids did I could tell some ashamed you, but stealing a clout round the ear by a copper was enough to behave. Whether its what your seeking for I dont know... PS Am an Ex Postman 1924–1959. Early Mornings Pd in winter we had an Oil Lamp we pined on an Uniform & the oil was colored Red, God help if you used any for own Bycle Lamp, if caught you would have been sacked and/or gailed by Stealing Government property, it was only in 1931 we got the change over to Electric Torches about same time as the Talkies came out on the screne

Apart from his piquant turn of phrase, it was immediately obvious that David's memories covered several decades. Henrietta Fanshawe, who also introduced herself by letter, made it clear that she thought the most interesting part of her life was the most recent. 'I am a mosaicist & have been working & teaching for 35 years (93). In the early 50's I went to the Chelsea School of Art followed by 20 years at Sir John Cass during which period I learnt to make mosaics from a Middlesbrough Professor – have continued in this field ever since including several exhibitions, the latest being in Dagenham (1992).' From the beginning, if sometimes diffidently, the potential contributors were suggesting what they themselves thought was interesting about their own lives. And it became increasingly clear that this had to be a major influence in choosing the programme themes for the television series.

There was another reason for this. Certainly the research effort by the team was impressively thorough. Trust needed to be established and this demanded special qualities in the researchers, beginning with a series of letters or phone calls, then a first visit, and then, when a contributor was identified, the development of an increasingly close relationship: some of the interviewers have ended up almost as family friends, sending flowers and notes for special occasions. But even such an effort was doomed to failure when we tried to tackle some themes, simply because there were no suitable contributors any longer alive. For the whole population of those over ninety still alive today is not a typical cross-section of their generation.

This is partly because, as survivors, they are obviously strong people, in body and in mind. But they are also overwhelmingly female   more than four women to every man – and probably two-thirds of them now come from middle- or upper-class backgrounds, whereas when they were young three-quarters of their contemporaries were working-class. The contrasts are even more startling when you consider particular occupations. The miners were the largest group of all workers in the early twentieth century, but the ravages of industrial disease have all but eliminated them from the over-nineties; today it is much easier to hear the voice of a tiny professional minority, like religious ministers.

So for lack of players, some themes were non-starters. And some had to be abandoned despite an especially intense search. An example is immigration, which was already a significant issue early in the century. After contacting some five hundred organisations in the Irish, Jewish, Afro-Caribbean, Chinese, German, Polish and Italian communities, it became indubitable that there were astonishingly few potential contributors among any of them. Often the few who had done much better had chosen to go back to their original homelands in retirement. For the majority who stayed, early struggle and continuing poverty had led to short lives. Here Ernest Marke speaks as a lone voice for those whose full story is already beyond the horizon.

The research effort could help the balance in some ways, bringing it closer to the past which was being remembered: for example, a third of the contributors are men. But there were absolute limits; and the narrower the focus, the more the difficulties. It is also very striking that although contact was made with very large numbers of homes for the elderly, there was only one from which any contributors were eventually chosen. Of the others, several live in self-contained sheltered accommodation with a warden at hand if they need help, but most live independently in their own small house or flat. The lack of voices from old people's homes is one stark measure of the extent to which institutionalised life saps the confidence of residents in themselves and their ability to speak. At ninety you still need to sustain your independence, even to keep the power of your own life story intact.

Keeping that power is indeed almost certainly one of the vital keys to well being in very old age. At any age, to keep healthy you need a sense of meaning and purpose in life, but as you get older that becomes still more important. Similarly, while at any age your memory is in a sense who you are (ask yourself what you could do if you had no memory), this becomes more obvious when you are less physically active. The contributors to *The Nineties* were certainly not inactive: they include not only a working mosaicist, but a working priest, an actor-entertainer still on stage, a working bookie, several writers and also continuing travellers. For many of them, life continues to be a discovery. But as the boundaries inevitably contract, so more and more it is the mind that matters. And as this book demonstrates, they have in their memories a resource of extraordinary richness.

Yet it is a little recognised wealth. Women usually live on their own and, in contrast to men, are as resilient alone as with a partner. Men mostly live with their wives, but find it hard to surprise them with their old stories. More important, both men and women have outlived almost all of their friends, their brothers and sisters (which makes the Summerhayes family so exceptional), and sometimes even their children. Most of them feel isolated in a world in which nobody seems interested in listening to them. Yet at the same time, the very fact that they have outlived nearly all their contemporaries seems to have changed what they are willing to tell. It was often almost as if the contact from the research team had come at the perfect moment. Once trust was established, the ninety-year-olds showed an astonishingly frank and down-to-earth candour to the young researchers, even to the point of telling personal stories which sometimes they had not shared with relatives or close friends. The researchers often felt they were being trusted with a very important responsibility. The contributors, despite their nervousness, visibly grew in their enthusiasm, excitement and renewed sense of their own significance. And even in a sense of mutual caring. Mary Butler wrote after being filmed: 'I do hope you got home safely on Wednesday last, and were not too tired after your long day. Thank you so very much for being so kind and interested in me and my life, what I feared might be rather an ordeal turned out to be a very happy afternoon. I do hope we meet again someday. Yours very sincerely, and with love...' The spirit of this letter perfectly captures the feeling on both sides. This mutuality was the foundation for the astonishing intimacy which is such a special quality of *The Nineties*.

It is also the secret to what is new about these still living memories from the horizon. Certainly they add nothing to what historians know about political history: they are not likely to mind whether or not the young David Taylor stood among the crowds watching Mrs Pankhurst and the suffragettes march through Manchester. It is also hard to find important new facts on many of the fundamental themes of social history: childhood and youth, poverty, housing, industrial work, the economy, or the impact of the First World War. There was a much wider range of people to call on when we were interviewing for *The Edwardians* twenty years ago. Today you can no longer hope to interview about married life in the 1900s, or working in the coal pits or in the fishing boats then, as was easy enough for us two decades ago. And while you can still interview about childhood, and also about poverty, the testimonies from ninety-year-olds today are most valuable to historians not because they say something different, but because they confirm just what seventy-year-olds were saying twenty years ago. That is important because it adds to our confidence in these memories. This was reinforced by the way in which the contributors, who were all recorded at least twice on different occasions, would repeat their accounts almost word for word. These testimonies are not only intimate, but consistent: they ring true.

What is new is more subtle. It is not so much the matter of the story, but the feeling which is expressed in it, the depth of candour, and also the reflection and in some cases the new perspective brought by living that much longer. In 'I Married a Stranger', for example, Lilian, Dorothy and George in particular speak about sex with an openness which would have been impossible when they were younger. Indeed it was impossible to record this kind of material twenty years ago. Older people have themselves been profoundly influenced by the changes in attitude among young people, with the result that they have reflected on their own earlier lives, and they are prepared to speak about them. But at the same time their own experience may still be changing. George's sadness in his first marriage is made infinitely more poignant by the fulfilment which he has found now.

There is a similar quality to 'All Your Kisses Are Mine', where Mary Butler tells how her father dominated her and ensured that she remained unmarried. Her story is a very painful one and she has wrestled with it all through her life. Mary only decided to speak out for the first time after much deliberation with her family. Like Joyce Wilkins, she reflects, from the perspective of very old age, on the sorrow of never having had children. Dorothy Galton, by contrast, was brought up by her parents to be an emancipated young woman, and never wished to sacrifice her independence through marriage. She belonged to a pioneering minority then. As an old feminist and socialist living in retirement in a very 'proper' village, she still felt part of a minority, but that made her all the more determined to put her experience on the record.

It is this same combination of private memories and reflection over a longer perspective which gives the special quality to other chapters. In 'The Demon in the Glass' Jenny Armstrong recalls the pub where she grew up, met and married her first husband, and had her first child; and you can set her private memories and regrets as a member of a publican's family along with those of Kate Garrett, whose parents met in a pub and scarcely ever left it. Kate married and emigrated to escape them, only to find that her husband in turn was an alcoholic. But she found her vocation thirty years later, as the *Daily Mirror*'s first 'Agony Aunt'. Donald Soper, by contrast, was brought up from childhood as a public campaigner against the 'demon drink', partly in reaction to a drunken grandfather. His own memories of a life-long campaign and on some of the mistakes which were made in it are the moment when the book comes closest to touching on public history, history with a capital H; yet again, it is his reflective openness which makes his interview so strong.

Again, in 'We Grinned and Beared It', Kathleen Norton and Colin Thomson are able to contrast the formidable powers of contemporary medicine with the sheer helplessness which they often felt as doctors faced with disease in the past. Remembering some of his earlier professional experiences in the steelworks slums of Rotherham still brings Colin to tears. Here too – and this is one of the characteristic strengths of oral history – we can set the story of the professionals against the experiences of the ordinary families who were their patients. The harrowing account which Charlotte Huggett gives of her own mother's mental illness was a terrible secret which she had kept buried inside her for seventy-five years. It is partly because attitudes to mental illness are changing, and partly because of her own point in life, that she was able to tell the story for the first time for *The Nineties*.

Our chapter 'Surf and Turf' gives a contrasting glimpse of the ways in which this generation found fun. It brings together material from the two programmes which were filmed last in the series, on Blackpool, the birth of mass holiday entertainment, and horse racing, which more than any other sport brought together devotees of all social classes. It conveys extraordinarily vividly how the magic of horses can engender a life-long passion, so that a ninety-year-old bookie will still take bets and an old jockey itch to be up in the saddle again.

The most astonishing tribute to longevity comes in 'And They Sailed Away', based on a family of six surviving brothers and sisters aged eighty-six to a hundred. They take us back in a time-capsule to the era when children were brought up on heroic stories of missionary-explorers like Livingstone and with a common ideal of service to the Empire. As children they dreamt of going out together to darkest Africa to help the natives, and as adults they scattered right round the globe to work as teachers, doctors and administrators: held together in spirit by the family myth which became the reality of their lives.

Finally, death. As one vicar, the Reverend Spriggs, remembered, 'In those days people spoke about death and not about sex. Nowadays, we can talk about sex and not about death.' But for many ninety-year-olds, death is not a taboo subject. Their stories are refreshing, eye-opening, at times funny and at times tragic. They range from the humour in the childhood familiarity with dead bodies which was so typical of the past, to Norman Collins' brutal honesty in describing mercy killing in the First World War trenches. In this chapter too, some of the contributors had never before been able to speak so candidly about their feelings about death, although all of them know that they now have little time left to live.

That was a reality not only for them, but for the team making *The Nineties*. Recapturing a history on the horizon made the schedules always vulnerable. Several potential contributors fell seriously ill or died shortly before being filmed for the programmes, while some others died in the months which followed. At ninety you cannot pretend any more about the brevity of human life. And the honesty with which the contributors face this is itself inspiring. Fear of dying in no way prevents them from making the most of life now, whether it be through watching and thinking, or writing poetry, or keeping up with politics, or listening to music.

The Nineties, in short, tells us a lot about being very old today. As younger generations, we expect too little of the very old. Care workers in institutions are too often content merely to get them out of bed every day. Young people are frightened of disturbing them by asking them difficult questions. Both ways, they are being treated as having lost their full human potential. But inside they still feel themselves as they always did. Some of them even feel young inside, and long to express their delight in naughtiness which they once shared with their contemporaries. And above all, they have the accumulation of decades of live experience. In drawing on that wealth for us, they not only take us back into a living past, poised on the horizon's edge, but they show us too the full humanity of living at ninety.

PAUL THOMPSON

1 I Married a Stranger

The generation who grew up before the First World War had to learn the facts of life the hard way. Certainly the seeds of the great change in attitudes to sexual relationships were already there. Havelock Ellis had begun to publish pioneering studies of sexual behaviour. Advanced radicals, feminists and socialists were proposing 'wild oats' for women as well as for men, trial marriage for engaged couples, an end to the 'double standard' in marriage itself by which adultery could be condoned for men only, and divorce for those couples who had ceased to love each other.

But such ideas were still utopian dreams. When our ninety-year-olds were young they could hardly have guessed that all this might come to pass within their own lifetimes. There were very few families then which dared to talk about sex. Even the poorest almost always took immense care, despite often sharing bedrooms and having to take their baths in turn in a tub in front of the kitchen fire, not to show their naked bodies to each other. You had to know German to read Freud: none of his work was yet published in English. Even Marie Stopes herself, the leading campaigner for the public birth control clinics which from the 1920s began to release women from the fear of pregnancy from every sexual encounter, grew up in extraordinary ignorance: although a young woman doctor, she lived for many months in an unconsummated marriage before discovering what was lacking in it. At that time very few mothers even warned their daughters about menstruation. Many young women believed that they could conceive through kissing and, even after marriage, that their children would be born through the navel.

Today, when sexual familiarity is the staple of public and private talk, it is hard to imagine a time when it was kept a dark secret. And at the same time there has been a profound change in the expectations of marriage itself. Certainly the ideal of love was always there, but it was seen as a hope rather than a right. The material basis of marriage, on the other hand, was seen as fundamental. A good husband was expected to earn enough to support wife and children on his wage alone. Although it was a generation since married women had ceased to be their husband's 'property' in strict legal terms, attitudes from that past time certainly lingered. In sharp contrast to today, most men and women formed sexual partnerships only well into adult life, and after marriage, typically in their late twenties. And most couples had fewer children than ever before, on average only two. Yet even so, a respectable wife was expected to give up paid work on marriage.

Our ninety-year-olds have lived through into a time when the taboos of their youth have fallen away, when a wife expects to keep a career in her own right, and when both men and women see a marriage which does not give them emotional and sexual fulfilment as a failure. Today they can not only talk about their personal experiences with a candour which is only now possible, they can also reflect, within a changing world, on the degree to which they allowed their parents to determine their lives. And on how they came to marry virtual strangers.

LILLIAN CHRISTOFAS *was born in Bristol in March 1896. She was the eldest child, and the only girl, with three younger brothers. Her father, 'a great scholar', was a tutor in Theological Studies at Clifton College, while her mother had 'a very gay social life of bridge parties and theatre outings'.*

They lived a comfortable upper-middle-class existence with a fleet of servants to help run their household. When Lillian was two years old the family moved to Hove, in Sussex.

It was the life of typical upper-class children: you had a nanny and you did exactly what Nanny told you. You got up, you washed and you were dressed, and you came down to breakfast. You said your prayers, and you stood behind your chair: you never, ever, ever, sat before Nanny sat. Nanny ruled the roost.

In the morning you went for your walks. We were very lucky, as we had a key to the private garden at the bottom of our road. The boys had a marvellous time. They could run with their hoops, they could do anything, even jump about on the seats; nothing was sacred to them. But I had to walk with Nanny by the side of the pram – be very careful not to get my white shoes dirty, not to let my socks get dirty, and keep my hands clean because I had white gloves on. That went on until you went home for lunch. Now the routine for a little girl was much the same for the boys. You took your street clothes off immediately, dress and all, and you got into your house clothes. Before you came to the table you put on your pinafore, so that your clothes were always kept spotless. Then you waited for Nanny to come into lunch. You stood, Nanny came in, and you sat down. Whatever food came up you had to eat. Oh! life was very, very strict.

God forbid if I spilled anything on me. I'd be punished very, very seriously. I used to go up, have to go upstairs in the dark and fetch Nanny down something she wanted, and that was a terrible ordeal because we had those gas mantles on the stairs and they made shadows on the wall. Oh that was dreadful – the shadow of a black man was on the wall and he was following me. Everywhere I went he came too. Of course I had no idea that it was my own shadow – a little girl, I didn't know.

Then I was told, 'Now when you go to tea, remember, you eat two things after your bread and butter and two things only. There'll be a cake on the table probably. If the cake is cut and you're offered some, you say "yes please" if you'd like it, and "thank you". If the cake isn't cut, you say "no thank you". And on no account must you ever say "yes please" if the cake isn't cut.'

It was also very important that a little girl learned carriage drill. You used to go to the stables where the carriages were and you learned carriage drill: that if there are three steps up, you take your right foot, your left foot, your right foot, and you go in the carriage on your left foot followed by your right foot, and you sit on the side where the carriage door is open. You learn it with two steps, three steps and four steps. When the carriage stops you must sit still. You must not move until the footman comes. He opens the door and he will give you his arm. You put your hand on it and come down. You must never stumble.

The boys had to stand if they were talking to a lady. Never, never sit. And take their hats right off, not just doff them as most men do. No, your hat right off, and your right glove if you're offered a hand to say 'how d'you do'. And the boys – they're like that to this day. It's in them – they can't help it. That's the way they were brought up and that's the way they behave.

I went to a very wonderful school when I was about twelve – real school. It was called Strathallen and it was a very, very private school for the daughters of professional gentlemen. Well, I didn't learn anything there – you learned to paint, you learned to play, you learned to sing and learned all the social graces that one had to know. But during my time there, something happened that altered my life completely.

My mother met a charming couple called the Brook-Taylors. Mrs Brook-Taylor was slightly eccentric; she loved cats and the Bible. They became very friendly and often came to my mother's 'At Home'. And there they saw me, because by now, I used to go in and hand the cakes round and learn the social graces that went on in those days at the 'At Homes'. After they visited a few times, they were madly in love with me. They had no children and they begged and implored to adopt me.

Well, of course, my parents wouldn't part with me, but they did say, 'If you like, you can have her to stay with you. You can have her in Hove or in London, whenever she's on holiday you can have her. So they very quickly had me. And it was the first time in my life I stayed up to dinner every night. It was wonderful. Then we went up to London and I was bought the most wonderful clothes; for the first time in my life I wore silk underwear. I had pure silk stockings and we went to a Court dressmaker. And then we went to Paris and that was marvellous. A lady's maid travelled with us. Soon after that, I was given a lady's maid of my own. We went to the couturier houses, and the great house then was Molyneaux, and I had a dress made for me by Molyneaux. My gloves were made to order at Perrins. You were measured and you chose your skins, you chose your silks, and all the buttons were little tiny balls of pearl that buttoned the gloves up; everything for your gloves, you chose, and they were made to measure.

We went everywhere. And of course we had the London Season, which was marvellous. I learned to dance properly because that was a social obligation. All young ladies had to really dance properly and I can remember how very strict the dancing mistress was about the waltz. I can hear her now: 'Right pass close, left behind turn. Right pass close, left behind turn …' It rings in my ears to this day and as soon as I get on the dance floor and it's an old-fashioned waltz, in my brain I'm singing, 'Right pass close, left behind turn. Right pass close, left behind turn …' I'll never forget it.

I went to Finishing School – only a term of it. It was a Catholic School, just outside Paris – and my father had arranged that I was *not* to go into Mass, I was *not* to go to Matins, and I was *not* to have a Catholic upbringing. They promised him that I wouldn't. But the promise wasn't kept. I was dragged up at six o'clock in the morning to go to Mass and after Mass another session of prayers, then in the bitter cold winter, go down and have a cold breakfast in a miserable cold room, with very little time given to lessons before there was more Chapel and more Matins and more prayers, and having to learn my Rosary. I've still got my Rosary by the way. I came home on holiday and I told them. I wasn't allowed to go back. So I escaped! And their only idea was to go there to perfect my French!

I called the Brook-Taylors Grandma and Grandpa. He was gentleman usher to His Majesty in his retirement, and she had been a lady in waiting. But now she was elderly and a little bit passé. Then he became our chargé d'affaires in Copenhagen where he became friendly with Queen Alexandra. I suppose that's how I came to be presented at Court, and presentation's the thing you remember all the days of your life. You never forget it. You didn't go down The Mall in a motor car in those days; there were no motor cars. You went down with two white horses, the same as you went to parties. I had a very charming escort and I was allotted into the Silver Room for supper. It was a very wonderful experience, making my bob to Queen Alexandra.

Life went on like that for quite a long time. Then one day my mother had a friend come to stay with her. She'd had a breakdown. Her son used to come and visit her. I was there and had no idea that he was enormously attracted to me. It didn't occur to me. I took no notice of him. I don't think I even liked him, but – he asked my father for my hand in marriage. I had no idea of it at all, not a clue. But I did think it was strange that this man was so terribly attentive to his mother, always coming to fetch her and see her. Of course he was coming to see me.

Then one day my father said to me, 'I want to see you in the study dear.' Well, I went in the study – that was nothing, I often went in the study – and he said, 'Edward' – called him Edward – 'Edward has asked for your hand in marriage.' 'My hand in marriage? I don't want to get married – I don't want to marry anybody.' 'Oh,' he said, 'you will. You are to marry him. It is a very, very good match. He's a nice man, a gentleman, an educated man. He's from a very good family and he's very well off. And I will be very happy to see you married to him. I can lay my head down when I've got to die, knowing you are well looked after.' I said, 'I'm not going to marry him.' He said, 'You will, you know. I'm telling you, you are going to marry him.' So my heart dropped and I thought, 'Oh my God.'... And I talked to my mother about it. She said, 'I'll try to talk father out of it. You haven't seen anybody. You're very, very young, too young to think of marriage. I don't approve at all. I quite

Lillian and her brother Pip, in 1915.

agree he's a very nice man, there's nothing the matter with him, but he's not for you dear. I shall talk to your father.'

Well, she talked to my father, but she might have talked to a brick wall. My father said I had to marry him, and I had to marry him. There was no argument about it. In those days, what your parents told you to do, you did. You didn't argue. I said, 'Oh how awful.' And he said, 'Don't let me hear you say that again. You'll have a very happy life. He'll be good to you, he'll take care of you' – and again – 'I will be able to lay my head down in peace knowing that you are looked after.' I never heard my mother raise her voice but she did shout at him about that. She said, 'You're making a very big mistake. That man is not for her. She hasn't seen anybody and it's not right that she should be bundled off to the first man who asks for her in marriage.' My father turned round and said, 'Will you please be quiet. You know nothing about these things.' My mother was so humiliated, because he said all that in front of me. I think she wanted the earth to open and swallow her up. I really do.

Well the next day, Edward arrived and I was brought into the drawing room. He stayed to lunch, and I was stuck with him. I hated it but I didn't say so. I thought, 'Well, this is ghastly, what am I going to do?' Nanny had gone, I couldn't discuss it with her. Our parlour maid, Florrie, was very friendly and she was very much one of the family, and she said, 'Well, Miss Lily, the only thing I can say is that it's the done thing. If your father says you've got to marry him, I'm afraid you'll have to.' Then she said, 'I wouldn't worry because, you know, once you're married you can do as you like. There's nothing you can't do.' She said, 'Perhaps I'll be able to come and be your lady's maid. We'll try and keep together so that I can see you're all right.'

I was told I was going to a film with this Edward and that he was going to propose and I had to say 'yes'. So we went to the cinema and we had a box, the only time I'd been alone with him. In the interval he went on his knees and proposed. I don't think I said 'yes', I'm sure I didn't, but he slipped a ring on my finger and said, 'Now we're engaged.'

From that moment onwards he sent me flowers, and chocolates, and bits of this and bits of that. He paid me so much attention. My family went to Tonbridge for a holiday and he came down for the weekend and asked if he might take me for a walk. This was the first time I'd ever been out alone with him, and we went for a country walk – my parents said for half an hour. We went over a field and there was a little stile we had to cross, and I wouldn't do it until he turned round and put his back on me. I was so shy; I was so prim. I was so afraid I might show my ankle or a little bit of my petticoat that I would not cross this very low stile until he turned round. He said, 'All right', and he turned round and I got over the stile, and I called out and said, 'I'm over.' He didn't seem shocked that I was so shy and so timid about it. Then he looked at his watch and said, 'It's time we went home.' And that's the only time I ever was out alone with him. So I didn't know him.

He used to visit us, have tea, and before I knew where I was the marriage was arranged. I was in a daze. We had the wedding, and I was so ill with nerves I don't know how I wasn't sick during the reception. I had diarrhoea too which was horrible. I couldn't travel, I was too ill, so we put up at the Metropole and had separate rooms, thank God! So that was my first night of marriage.

The next day we travelled in the Brighton Belle to London and my troubles started. I went into it like a lamb to the slaughterhouse. I hadn't the faintest idea what an adult man had down there. He was very highly sexed and I didn't know anything about sex. I had seen my brothers running about in the bathroom and I had seen they'd got a bag of tricks in front of them, but I thought nothing of it. They used to say to me, 'Aren't you lucky, yours is tucked in!' I mean, I didn't know there was such a thing as erections. I didn't know that a man dug that awful thing into a woman. I had no idea of anything like that. I was in a state of terror, in a state of physical agony, and I went through the tortures of hell. I never got over it. I used to talk to my old girlfriends, who had got married, about it and they used to say, 'You know, it isn't so bad once you get over the pain of it. It isn't too bad once you get over the nasty part of it. In fact, sometimes it's quite comforting. You don't want to worry, it'll come to you.'

It never came to me. It was the nightmare of my life. I used to go home and cry to my mother, and she said, 'Well, darling, I'm afraid that's what marriage is about.'

I said to my father, 'I must have a divorce.' He said, 'Divorce? Have you gone mad? Do you know what you're saying?' I said, 'Yes, I can't live like this.' I said, 'I can't stand it. Married life is too terrible.' I said, 'It's the most awful thing. I think it's shocking.' And he said to me, 'What do you mean, shocking? You've got everything you want. You've got a motor car, you've got a maid, you've got servants, you've got a beautiful house. What more do you want?' I said, 'To be left alone.' And he said, 'You'll get used to it. That's marriage. You'll get used to it.' I said, 'I never will.'

Edward used to say, 'I don't know what you're making a fuss about. It's all a natural thing and everybody does this in married life. What are you crying for and what are you making a fuss about? If you'll only give yourself up and not be so tense, you'll quite like it.' And I said, 'Never, never!'

I suppose the truth is I was a frigid woman, because I wasn't taught anything, you see. When you're a virgin you need a lover to woo you and to show you the ropes and make you want him. I didn't have any of that. I mean it was just like a bull in a china shop. I didn't have any preliminaries. Nothing.

I don't think it would have been any trouble at all if I had been in love with the man. I think it was the fact that he was a stranger to me. I mean, put yourself in my place. Just imagine going to bed with a strange man who jumps on top of you and digs into you with a great big pole. I'm buried, with this lump – pushing into me on top of me, and all I'm doing is biting my mouth in torture and trying not to scream out. It's terrifying. I didn't know men were made that way. I'd no idea. Nobody told me anything and I think it's wicked. If ever I had a daughter, the first thing I'd do when she was old enough, I'd tell her all about it.

I think he was a virgin. I think he only knew he had to dig into me and I bled, oh so badly, and I was so sore. I had wounds because I wasn't a big girl and he was a big man. Well, at least he was big in that department. And, very fierce. I don't know how I didn't come to have children. That's an extraordinary thing, because usually a virgin's given a child – bang, pop – right away. But it didn't happen to me, and I'm very pleased about that because I don't know what I'd have done.

Well let's face it dear, he married me to go to bed with me, I know that. I know it now. I didn't know it then. I didn't understand it then. There was no ending to this physical part of the marriage. It was dreadful. I hated it, I loathed it. And of course, dear, I realise now that I have had a lot of experience of life, I realise a marriage can't be right if the bed's wrong, and mine was very wrong. So of course the marriage was wrong too.

The First World War gave Lillian a second chance. She and Edward married in 1915, two years into the war, and before long he was called to the front. He returned mortally sick from the effects of poison gas. 'He died, and I was free.'

In the meantime Lillian had also lost her mother. 'It was a great blow to me and a great sorrow. And my father, when I became widowed, said I should go back to live with him, and I did. I went to live with my father and with Nanny. I had a lovely old Nanny. We lived with my father for two years, and I was very, very happy.' But then Lillian's father 'suddenly announced he was going to marry', a 'shocking' choice. 'My mother would have been horrified, because her brothers were in trade. She was horrible, that's all I can tell you. And she said to my father, "Your daughter can't live with me. We can't have two mistresses of the house."'

Lillian's father had a solution in mind, but this time Lillian was no longer prepared to be forced. 'I had met somebody again, who my father wanted me to marry. And I was determined. Once bitten, twice shy. I was determined not to marry him.' This time, however, fortune was also on her side, for the rejected suitor had a friend.

He was Greek, so my father was very, very against it. But he won my father's heart. I had a wonderful marriage for over fifty years. It was love at first sight and the same thing happened with him. He looked at me and he said to himself, 'That's the girl I'm going to marry.' I didn't know about love, dear. It hadn't come my way. But I looked at him and I knew I loved him.

Lillian is now a widow for the second time, living on her own in Haywards Heath, Sussex. She has an active social life. Until recently she was still driving her car, but had to give up because of increasingly frail health. She keeps in touch with her only surviving brother, who lives in Australia – every Saturday they telephone to talk.

GEORGE WALTER CURETON *was the son of a policeman who died when George was seven years old. Born in 1901 in Staines, Middlesex, he was one of a close-knit family of three boys and four girls. When he was eight, he was sent away from home to the Police Orphanage at Strawberry Hill, Twickenham, for his education. George remembers how he felt at this time:*

I was the one selected really. My younger sister Bertha was eighteen months older than me. My mother thought Bertha's character would have made the orphanage very, very difficult for her. She was more likely to kick over the traces than I was. I don't suppose I could kick anybody. All the rest were too old.

I loved my home, we were a real family. My eldest sister was extremely kind to me. We all liked each other. We got along very well, and I enjoyed the life that I was living. I didn't want to go and leave everybody. I'd sooner have gone to prison. The thing I missed altogether was any form of affection. It was march in for dinner, march in to tea, march in to breakfast. March here, march there, fall in, fall out.

We had about half as many girls as we'd got boys, and we never spoke to each other. It wasn't allowed. If a boy had a sister there he wasn't allowed to speak to her. Nobody was unkind, but nobody bothered to be very kind either. Perhaps they hadn't got time, I don't know. But there was no affection whatsoever, and I – I'm afraid I always wanted a little affection during my lifetime. Still do, haven't changed. Well, I think for the first couple of years I cried myself to sleep nearly every night.

But I eventually got to the stage where I accepted the old adage, 'What cannot be cured must be endured', and that's how I went along. It was part of my life. There was nothing I could do to change it. Make the best of it.

When my father was alive he was a very, very efficient provider. When he died they cut his allotment into three and gave it to three other fellows. He grew everything he wanted. There was quite a good deal of bartering done in those days. The average copper was able to do a good turn here and a good turn there, get a leg of pork and that sort of thing. And we did very well thank you. He was a very good provider.

When he died, my mother had got nothing. She didn't work. She was an extremely good needlewoman, but she'd got four daughters. The only place in Staines where they could work was the Middlesex and Surrey Laundry, and as in every other place in the world, and definitely in this country, if there was a bountiful supply of labour and not many places to be filled, the wages come down. I believe my sisters got a maximum of about three and six a week for packing in the laundry. The stuff they had to pack was very largely the stuff that came from Buckingham Palace. Every single hamper had to have every layer in perfect order, almost plumb line and spirit level. Each member of the Royal Family had a vast laundry basket of their own and then of course there was an enormous amount of linen for the household. So what with Windsor and Buckingham Palace, that laundry could have managed very well on the royal bounty. But my sisters wouldn't have managed very well on the wages. And my mother couldn't live on it.

You see, in those days there was no widow's allowance, no children's allowance. Mother's main job was to keep the family together, because if they'd have gone in the workhouse, the girls would have gone one way, the boys would have gone another, and we should have been broken up. So mother immediately got herself in gear and did what she could to keep the place going.

Her father, who lived in Birmingham, suggested that the thing to do was to pack all her house up, move up to Birmingham, and he'd find plenty of work for 'em up here. So that's what they did. I was in the orphanage. I was left there while everybody else came up to Birmingham. I suppose they were financially better off, because they could get better jobs, slightly better pay and that sort of thing.

I was nearly fifteen when I left the orphanage, and I was just turned sixteen when I joined the Navy about twelve months later, or fifteen months later. If we remained in the same employment for twelve months after we'd left school we got a whole guinea. But I never got mine. I couldn't stick in the job. So I didn't get my guinea but I got in the Navy instead. Got myself a fourteen-year job.

George became a radio operator in the new submarine service. He was in his mid-twenties when he met Edith, and they courted for another eight years after that.

The whole of my family, my mother and sister, my brother's wife, they were all in the rag trade. My sister at that time had a small business making children's clothing and she had my first wife Edith working for her. Most of them belonged to a Methodist church and to the tennis club down here. So that's where I met Edith. She didn't live far away, and we used to play tennis together – always meeting at home when she'd finished work. And we got to know each other, as it were. And that's all there was to it.

I wouldn't get married while I was still in the Navy. I didn't see any sense in trying to run a home on what I was getting then. Our

George, aged seventeen, after joining the Navy.

courtship, if you like, was always done at a distance of anything from one to twelve thousand miles, and writing letters, that sort of thing. You can't get too excited writing a letter at twelve thousand miles can you? I was home on leave, what, four nights at the most at a time, unless I came from abroad and then I might get a bit longer. But we didn't have long periods together.

I don't know that we ever did anything very exciting together as a matter of fact. We were very, very circumspect. Very. She used to come to my home of a Sunday to tea and that sort of thing, and I would go to hers to tea. And we'd go to the pictures together and occasionally to the theatre if we'd got some money, but not often. Not very exciting. We were, for the first five years, or six years anyway, more or less strangers to each other, because I was either in Hong Kong or somewhere like that and she was in Birmingham. So we didn't spend all that much time together.

George finally left the Navy and became a radio shop assistant before he and Edith married in 1933.

We were married in a church. I don't even know which church. I can't remember a thing about it. We were just not suited. She had no sense of humour. Edith had various little ways of showing anybody I brought home, she more or less indicated, that they weren't very welcome. So I didn't bring people home. It was just one of those things. So I'd sit at home with a book. Well, I very soon discovered that I'd got the wrong idea of marriage altogether. At least I'd got a very different idea to that of my wife. There was no, what shall we say, sexual relationship at all. My wife was evidently not interested. And after being very, very patient, I think I came to the conclusion it was no good knocking my head against a brick wall for ever. So I decided to pack it in. But not to the point of getting a divorce or anything of that sort.

I thought, 'Well, she doesn't want me,' and to really strain and struggle at sex with somebody who doesn't want it is not conducive to pleasure. So I decided to really not try any more. I suppose that would be about six or seven years after we were married. Our marriage went on for forty-three years and I never touched her. I don't think I ever got really near enough to her to develop a real loving relationship. We lived together in this house, and the one before, and we just got along. We had our meals together. We changed to single beds and we just, I suppose, put a face on. Nobody seemed to know that there was anything wrong at all. So I left it at that.

It was very early on in our marriage when she shouted across the room at me, rather loudly and rather nastily, I thought – 'What are you staring at?' Well, she was rather a nice looking woman, and we were going to bed, she was getting undressed – I didn't know I was staring. If I was, I suppose I'd got something to stare at. Anyway, I took offence at the remark and I said, 'You'll never speak to me like that again.' And as a consequence for the rest of our married life, that was the best part of forty years, I went upstairs after she'd got into bed, got undressed in the dark and got in bed. We had separate beds by then, and that's how we arranged things. So I was never in the room when she was dressing or undressing.

Even now I put everything in exactly the same place, so that I can find them in the dark if I want 'em. It's not much trouble. Every night, I take my glasses off and my wrist watch. I keep a handkerchief in my dressing-table drawer, put my glasses and my watch on it. And I've done that every night, so I can find them in the dark. Easy.

I had given a marriage what I considered to be a fair trial. I had tried to discuss this matter of personal relationships, but I was always shut up from the very, very first word. 'We don't talk about that.' And that was that. Can't make somebody listen if they don't want to. There wasn't that much I could do about it. Well, I had thought about leaving, but in every case I thought, 'Who is going to be upset by this? – my mother, my sisters, my brother, her parents.' I didn't see any reason why I should upset a lot of people over something that was my fault. I married her in any case. So why should I make everybody else unhappy about it?

Yes, I would have liked children. Yes. Still, I could always get plenty by going out and doing my front garden. Every time I went out there the kids used to come in and talk to me.

Divorce wasn't for the likes of me. I couldn't afford it. It's still the same today isn't it? If you look round, people who get divorced are people who've got money. Lloyd George – if he'd have got caught he'd have had hundreds of divorces wouldn't he! No, I wouldn't know how to go about it. You've got to go through all the strain of going to court, going through a solicitor. It wouldn't do me, wouldn't do me at all.

Well my first, Edith, she died almost precisely eighty years of age – just a week over her eightieth birthday. She always made a big fetish of eightieth birthdays and she went into hospital just before her eightieth birthday.

George has found deep happiness and satisfaction in his second marriage to Freda, made the following year when he was already in his late seventies. He had known Freda, who was born in 1915, for many years already, since she had first worked as a young needlewoman for his mother and sister. Later she joined their family holiday parties. Today they are a close couple, sharing their pleasure in music, crosswords, gardening, and each other's company.

I'd known Freda by meeting her at my mother's home. I got to know her by just seeing her round the house. You see Freda was something that grew. We both liked music. She had a very, very nice voice. She was always good company. She would chat and talk and laugh. I'd got to admire her qualities. We were on the same level in many other ways.

Anyway, my sister and Freda moved in here and when Edith died, well, I said to Freda, I said, 'We've known each other for a long time. Would you like to get married?' And we got married straight away – much too quick for some of the neighbours I expect. But anyway we got married and that's all there was to it. We had drifted into a close, caring position and I thought then, and I think now, that she's got every good quality I can think of and no bad ones.

We've got something between us that I didn't even know existed. That's what we've got. Because my life had been what it was before, it makes it ten times better than ever. We thoroughly enjoy life together. And I'm ninety – over. The urge is no longer about, but I still worship the ground she walks on. When we married we thought we might be lucky if we got four years. So this is all overtime, good overtime. Most of my colleagues where I worked, always every time they went in, they'd have a look round to see how much overtime they could get. I never did. I hated overtime. But I like this.

DOROTHY SPENCER *was born in Leicester in 1901. Above her were three brothers and one sister. She grew up not knowing her father, who left the family home after his father-in-law bought him out of both his share in the family bakery business and his marriage – 'she got rid of him'. Dorothy's mother did much of the baking herself: 'bread and tarts and everything, all home-made. She ran the business very profitably.' She controlled her family too with a very firm hand, but she also had a love of music and fun. She had a great influence on Dorothy.*

My mother was a very strong-willed woman and she was a suffragette to the core. She employed three men in the bake-house, two assistants in the shop, and we had a maid for the house. Women didn't have a vote then and she used to say over and over again, 'I've got those five men that I employ, and they all depend on me. They get a vote, I don't.' And she said, 'I've got all the brains and they haven't.' She'd go on about this, and I think she was right.

But she was strict. She had to be. She'd got three boys and two girls to bring up, and no man to help her. And running the business as well. She was a really wonderful person in lots of ways. She said it was her duty: a) to educate us well, which she did – we all went to grammar schools; b) to clothe us well; c) to feed us well; d) to teach us good manners. At the table we really had to behave, there was no doubt about that. But as a mother, she never took me on her knee. I don't remember her cuddling me or anything. And yet I knew that she did care for me and the others. I knew she loved me but she couldn't show it. She was brought up as an only child in a very stiff atmosphere.

But when I went to the grammar school and made friends, I went to their houses a lot, and they all had fathers. And you know, it was much freer; because if you've got a business and a home, the business always comes first. It's got to. I realised that, so I never had quite the same comforts that the other children did. You know, running around a house and so on. And I would have liked to have had a father. You see he went, he left, or she turned him out, I don't quite know how it happened, but my grandfather bought him out, so that my mother could have the business and run it. He bought it for her. And so my father never came back. I saw him once when I must have been about five. He had a beard, I can see it now, and I thought he was rather nice. I missed having a father.

But I was happy. I was never unhappy. Never. And I think it was due to the fact that I was the youngest. When I was born my mother was dying to have a girl. She was very naughty because she did make a pet of me. I'd got a lot in common with her. We were close because she loved music and she played the piano and sang. So that's why I suppose I always, I was always happy.

Dorothy's first husband, Ted, owned a rope factory.

I met him at a dance. A hockey dance. As I walked into the dance room, he was with another man, and he said to this man, 'Who is she?' I was introduced to him, and that is how I came to know him. And from then on, when he called, I went out with him. We did the usual rounds that they did in those days, dances and dinner dances, visiting, and all that.

He was a partner in his own business and he'd got plenty of money. He was quite well-to-do, and of course all these things, I suppose, mattered in a way. I think one of the things that may have attracted me to him as well was that I was brought up to have extremely good manners, and he was very, very well mannered. What you would call 'gentlemanly'. Raise his bowler to you and standing up if a woman came into the room. His manners were perfect.

He was a boxer, amateur boxer. He was very keen on that. He was very fond of the country, and I loved it. So we went out together, but all he had eyes for, 'Would this be good shooting ground? Or hunting ground?' Because he had his hunter. And he had his guns. He hired a shoot, booked two large fields, for shooting. He took me with him. But when he saw a rabbit, I used to jump up and clap my hands to frighten it away, so he wouldn't get it. Of course he got furious with me. This sort of business went on, and in the end I didn't go shooting with him.

Another thing he did was to go fishing in the pond belonging to the farm. He caught this fish, and put it on the ground and, you know, when it's first out of the water it's fighting for its life; it wriggles. And I said to him, 'Aren't you going to kill it or something?' He said, 'No, it's all right.' 'Well,' I said, 'if you're not, I am.' And I threw it back in the water, so that it would live. And he was so wild he pushed me into the pond. After the fish!

Anyway, his mother became ill, very ill, and they knew she wouldn't get better. She hadn't long to live. He said, 'I want you to come up and see her.' So I went to see her and she said to me, 'I want you to promise me that you will marry Ted.' Well, I'm sure she must have had an inkling too that I was cooling off. But she said this and I couldn't say no. When a person is lying in bed like that, and you know they're not going to get better and they're dying, what do you do?

Anyway, I said, 'Yes, I will.' And of course that promise was on my conscience all the time. So much so that, honestly, when we were being married I nearly ran away. I had the feeling I shouldn't be doing this – I shouldn't be doing this: it was wrong. Now if you're going to start off on that premise, you're not going to be successful really, are you? I went through with it, as you know, but I do blame myself to a great extent. But I think if I hadn't made that promise to his mother, I would have broken it off before.

I knew nothing of sex. In my home it was never mentioned at all. And at my grammar school I never knew a girl to be pregnant and if she was, I probably wouldn't have noticed. I didn't know where babies came from when I was seventeen. So that everything that happened after came as a bit of a shock, because I didn't really know what it all entailed, you see. I hadn't thought of bed at all.

My wedding night wasn't very successful because I didn't want to take my clothes off. But he took all his clothes off. I'd never seen a man like that before, naked, and I felt a shock. I thought I wanted to get into the wardrobe and shut myself in it. I think he should have taken – a different line. I mean, he knew I'd not been with a man at all before, that I'd not seen a man. And that did come as a shock. I think if we could have, say, broken into it gently, sort of bit by bit. Somehow, I don't know how, but not just straight into it like that, you know what I mean? That is the part that upset me right at the beginning.

For the first few months it wasn't too bad. He was very keen on bridge and we used to have a few bridge parties. By the way, I hated bridge, but we used to entertain a little. Then eventually all this seemed to stop, and I suppose the friends we knew began to see that things were certainly not what they should be between us. The way we were behaving together. It was all really hopeless.

Dorothy enjoying herself on the beach at Bognor, Sussex, in the summer of 1928, six years after she had left her husband.

I was earning my own living before I married and I had my own money. But when I married him, no. He handed it out to me like he'd given a sweet to a child. I felt I wasn't a free person. That was it. I wasn't free to do as I liked. And there was nothing about him that was – gentle, if you know what I mean. I mean, he wasn't gentle with his animals. he had no love for any of his animals. They had to do what he wanted. He'd whip his horse on, his dog had to bring in the birds he'd shot or the dog was no good. And this seemed to be instilled in him. He didn't have a gentle touch. At all.

I wouldn't go to bed with him in the end. I thought, I really thought, deeply, 'I can't bring a child like him into the world.' I thought if I have any children, and one is like him, it would be awful. He used to – hit me – because I wouldn't go to bed with him. Now, you see, he regarded me right from the beginning as his property. I was there to do his bidding, so to speak. But I'm not that sort of person. So when I wouldn't go to bed with him, this is what caused the trouble. Then he started to knock me about a bit. There was one episode, he got out his gun. And he said he was going to shoot me. I can remember the feeling, 'Oh very well.' So I said, 'Well, go on and do it if you want to.' And that was all I said. He put the gun down and he said, 'You won't be worth hanging for.'

Anyhow, I went out one day. I think it was to a river. I sat on the bank and I said to myself, 'I'll have to leave him. But what can I do?' Because in those days a woman didn't leave her husband. They always thought there must be something wrong with her, you know, to do a thing like that. It can't be the husband who's wrong. It must be the woman. Because the women in those days, they put up with all these things. Sometimes if the man wasn't as nice as he should be, you just put up with it. So it's always that the woman was in the wrong. But if the husband left his wife, then it didn't matter half as much. He could go about and do his business and do what he liked. But the woman couldn't.

Anyway, I thought it out. I thought first of all, 'What can I do?' I could commit suicide. Well, obviously I'm not going to do that, I love living. Secondly, I should have to get a job, and to get a job I've got to go somewhere. My mother was dead against me leaving him, so I could not stay at home. I can't understand my mother taking his side, because she did what I did, in a way. But you see she was brought up in this Victorian 'Forsyte Saga' way, where when a man marries you, you're his property. And my husband really did think that. I was his property, but he could just do as he liked. She said, 'You're throwing everything away. Everything for your future.' So I said, 'I don't want it.' So all I was left with was to get a job as soon as I could, and keep myself. And that is what I did. I left him.

Now, he wouldn't give me any money, at all. Ever. So what I did, I knew where he kept his. There were a set of drawers in the house, and they were awfully nice – I'm sure they were probably old or something – but he kept it locked, so that I couldn't help myself. So when he was out I got a screwdriver and I pushed it in this drawer and wriggled and wriggled and forced it open. And I took all his money. Every bit that was there. I felt it was owed to me.

So I was able to get away, and plan, and live until I got a job. When I left my husband and had to keep myself, I went after jobs and they didn't want to employ me, just because I was married. When I got this money, I could get on to the train to London to get a job. I did away with my wedding ring altogether and I called myself Miss.

I went to my solicitor and he said you can't get a divorce unless you can prove adultery and cruelty. 'Well,' I said, 'I can prove cruelty but I don't know anything about adultery. I don't think he's done it or anything' – and, I said, 'I'm not going to. I've no intention of providing him with adultery.' But in the end he gave in, and went to this hotel in London and was photographed in the hotel bedroom in bed with a woman. The woman was the barmaid who'd been paid. Now this is a dreadful thing to happen, but that's what had to be done. Simply for the law to be able to say that the man was in bed with this woman. It forced people to commit some sort of adultery. To get a divorce.

If he'd started out by being a generous, kind person, it might have made a lot of difference. I might have grown to care for him in some way. But his manner after we were married seemed to make life very, very hard. I'd been a free person, and a happy person. I'd had my own way, and I was never accustomed to being regarded as below him in intellect or anything. My mother had brought me up to believe that women were more intelligent than men and I went through life thinking much more of women than I did of men. But then, with him, I had to put all those ideas away. I wasn't anybody in my own right. I had no rights.

You should be happy in your life, for life's too short to carry on without happiness. I'm not a miserable person by any means and I love laughing. But to be, sort of tied down and held, so that I couldn't be my real self, I couldn't bear it. I wanted, I wanted the freedom I had before I married him, which he took away from me.

Dorothy worked as a secretary after her divorce and in 1931 she married Dick, who worked in his father's bookshop in London and was a few years younger than her. They have been happily married for sixty-one years and have had three children – two boys and a girl. They both love music, gardening and the countryside. 'He is the very exact opposite to my first husband in every possible way. He is kind and thoughtful and he makes me laugh. And he is ever so generous too, so it really worked out well.'

EDITH SMITH *is the youngest of three children, and was born near the docks in Deptford, London, in 1901. When she was three years old her father, a Scandinavian sea captain, died at sea after a fight on board ship.*

Well the next thing my mother was wondering was how she was going to keep us, bring us up. She was a school teacher and in those days they were not allowed to work after they were married. So the question was, what was she going to do? With three little children? Anyway, she saw there was a factory very near where you could apply for work – you could work at home – and she thought, 'Well that's the only thing I could possibly do.' Being a Norwegian she was very good at sewing and they said, 'Well, it's finishing work.' Little tiny pieces of cotton that were sewn in the trousers. She took them home. That was the way she kept us. And what she got from selling the furniture. We lived in one room. It was just bare boards, you know.

My mother had to manage on four and six a week. She had rent to pay out of that, and she had to keep us in clothing. You know it's cheap to buy the things and make them, but you couldn't make shoes. And very often we couldn't go to school because we had no shoes. That was really poor in those days, very poor. There was no dole money. You couldn't apply for it; the only thing that they would do, would be to take the children away and put them in a home. Well, no way would my mother do that. She would rather struggle and work all hours of the night. That was why she sent me to school so young, about three, because she thought

she could do more work without me being at home. Well after about a year, my small brother died. He had diphtheria that was very prevalent in those days among children. Whether that was a blessing, I don't know. But it meant that was one less to keep, one less to bring up.

I must have been about eight when my mother met a man called Chris Beacham, who'd lost his wife in childbirth. He was a very lonely kind of man and they got friendly and he used to visit us. After about maybe a year, as far as I can remember, they were married. Because there was no birth control, nothing at all that one knew about, she had ten children after that, one after another. So that the poor soul had no life whatever. As soon as she finished breast feeding one baby she was pregnant again with another. Some died; some died when they were very young, you know, a few months old. One I think died at seven. Another one died at twenty-one. But there were tragedies all through it seemed to me.

I think I was nineteen when she had the last, a little girl, and I was still living at home. I was useful at sewing but my job at home was to look after the babies, while she worked again. You see it was a continual work period for her. The only time that I remember things being easier was in the First World War. Because he had to go into the army, and then my mother had the money from the government. So that was the only time I can ever remember that things were fairly easy. Otherwise it was a struggle all the time.

I must have been eleven or twelve, and things were so tight that she had to apply for me to have meals at school, which if people were very poor, they could have free. I remember the humiliation I felt, going to school to have breakfast. It consisted of two pieces of bread and jam and a cup of cocoa, and the dinner was always a stew of some kind. But I can feel now the humiliation, you know, of all my school friends knowing that my mother was too poor to feed me.

Well, as the babies arrived, Chris Beacham, he made lovely chairs, he thought he would start up on his own. And he had a lathe, hand planes and chisels – we had a scullery which he used there. He made the frames of the chairs, and then he'd do all these lovely little inlays in the back and at the top. It was fascinating to watch him. This is how I came to love wood. I loved ebony, and rosewood and satinwood that he used all the time. But it was a terrible living trying to sell them. I can remember him putting the chairs on a barrow and walking from Bethnal Green, where we lived, up to the West End to Waring and Gillows or one of those big shops up there, trying to sell his lovely chairs. And then wheeling them all the way back again when he didn't. I did wonder why my stepfather could never sell those lovely chairs he made. It was a hard life altogether and it never seemed to get any better.

I loved going to school but I went so very little. I was the one who had to look after the babies, you see, while my mother worked and tried to make more money. When I was thirteen and a half I was offered a job. My mother was working at a tailoring place and they said that I could have a job if I wanted it. And that meant four and sixpence extra a week. So I left school.

The job was in a basement room. To soap seams of men's coats, men's jackets. There was a huge iron that you had to heat by putting it against the stove, and then you put it into a kind of tin casing, because you couldn't really let the hot iron go on the cloth, you see. I worked from eight o'clock in the morning till six at night; thirteen and a half, for four and sixpence a week. They were tough times, they were really tough times. I was never allowed out to play.

When I was fourteen, I was allowed to work properly – that was the legal age when you were allowed to work. Well, I saw advertised a job: they were taking on learners to make brushes and this was in Clapton, East London. Mind you, it was a three-mile walk, but I walked there and I walked back. Well, I didn't, I skipped. If I had a skipping rope I could get along quicker. So I skipped all the way there and all the way back. And I learned how to make brushes.

I used to walk to work with a girl, she was a Jewish girl and her father kept a shop. One day she said, 'Would your mother allow you to come out?' Mind you, I was eighteen then. So I said to my mother, 'Could I go out?' and she said 'Well, yes.' She let me go.

Well, the thing is that there used to be a parade, Mare Street, Hackney. All the girls used to parade in pairs, the boys used to parade in pairs. However this particular Saturday night we were walking along, and a couple of boys came towards us. The one on my side was the very fair boy. And the one on her side was the very dark boy. So, you know, with everything being even, I should have gone to the fair boy, and she should have gone to the dark boy. But somehow we crossed over, so that I got the dark boy and she got the fair boy and we were absolute contrasts! Anyway we got chatting about one thing and another and

Edith grew up in Bethnal Green. She was not allowed to mix with other children in case she picked up a cockney accent.

he said, 'Do you like reading?', and I said, 'Oh yes.' I had discovered books when I was quite young and so we talked about books. He wanted to take me out on the holiday Monday – wanted me to go to Epping Forest. I said, 'Oh I don't really know whether I would be allowed to.' So he said, 'Would you ask your parents if you can come out with me?'

Well, it wasn't only a question of going out with him but, you see, we bought our clothes on the 'never never'. We bought the things and paid a shilling a week for them. But in our house, things were so tight, that every Monday morning when I wore my clothes to go to work, my best costume was taken to pawn, to pay the rent, you see. I thought, 'Well, how am I going to get to go out, without my good costume?' And, 'How am I going to ask my mother if I can have my costume on Monday morning, to go out? – even if she'd let me go out with a boy.'

However, I talked to her and I said, 'I've met a very nice boy, I think you would like him.' And I said, 'He lives fairly near.' I said, 'He asked me to go out on Monday. He wants to take me to Epping Forest,' She said, 'Well, I don't like the sound of that.' However, she did let me go and she let me wear my costume. She pawned it on the Tuesday.

But he was a very bright lad, he made me laugh, and then we went out together. He took me to the Hackney Music Hall, where they have different turns. All sorts of different people came on, like a man called Max Miller, and then he would imitate these people, you know, and he made me laugh. I had to be in at half past nine though. I couldn't be in later than half past nine. Why we couldn't get up to mischief before half past nine, I don't know!

But the place where we lived, I wouldn't never, ever, let him come. I would never ever let him see me home, because it was down a little cutting, down a little alleyway. At the end of this cutting there was a glass-blowers' place, and the loo that we had was out in the yard. As the glass-blowers was warm, they got a lot of cockroaches in there, which used to come into our house. Well, I had no bedroom. I had to sleep in the living room on a little camp bed. And as I went to sleep all these cockroaches used to crawl up the wall. I could hear them all scrabbling about and I used to put my head under the sheets and hope I could go to sleep. And I often wonder whether that was the cause of me not sleeping well, for I was woken up so many times by these things I think being awake became second nature to me. It wasn't very good, wasn't good.

One night he took me home and he wanted to make a fuss of me, and I said, 'You can stop that.' So he said, 'Well, what's the matter?' He said, 'I've been going with a girl in Brighton, she let me do that.' I said, 'Right, you go back to the girl in Brighton, I'm going home.' So I took myself home, I wasn't having anything like that.

I think I was a little bit concerned because I knew nothing. Nobody had told me anything. Mothers didn't seem to tell children anything in those days, no idea of what went on, but I had my mother's experiences of having a baby every year. The feeling was that if I let a man touch me, you know, I'd end up like she was. And that's the last thing I wanted.

When the war was over, Chris Beacham got a job, woodworking in a factory. And then they used to have a drink, occasionally. My poor mother was the kind of person who if she had half a pint of beer, she would get aggressive. And she got really aggressive towards me. I could never do anything right. But he used to buy the beer, in a jug you see, and bring her half a pint home. And she'd drink it and immediately she'd get aggressive and life became pretty well unbearable.

Anyway this went on for some years. Things were very bad at home and I really had had enough of it. I went out that Saturday and I was in tears and Fred said, 'Have you been having a bad time again?' And I said, 'Yes.' He said, 'Right!' He said, 'Do you think we can make a go of it?' He never said he loved me or whether would I marry him. All he said was, 'Do you think we can make a go of it?' And I said, 'Well I suppose so.' And he said, 'Right, we'll go and see the vicar and we'll put the banns up. The earliest we can be married is two weeks,' he said, "cos the banns have to be called three times. They can be called tomorrow, and then the next two weeks and that would bring us up to Whit Monday.' And he said, 'We can be married in the morning of Whit Monday. Is that all right with you?' I said, 'Yes, I suppose so.'

Edith was then nineteen. On her wages and Fred's as a Stock Exchange clerk, they rented two rooms from a landlady. Edith was wearing a ring they had bought in a pawnshop.

I just walked out. Never told a soul. I never told my mother where I was going. She knew I'd gone off with him, but I never told her where I was going or where I was living. It was almost impossible to follow me. Really I had had enough of it. My great aim in life was to have a bedroom of my own.

For my wedding morning I put on my best costume, which was brown, the one that I had to wait to get out of pawn if I wanted to go anywhere. I had a pair of white gloves and I had a white hat, which possibly cost me two shillings. And that was the wedding outfit. No flowers, no buttonholes, no bells, no organ, no anything. Just the four people in the church. Just the service as usual, you know. And that was it. Then we went home to our wedding breakfast, which was a tin of salmon, red salmon mind you, best salmon we had, half a pound of tomatoes and some bread and butter. And then the other people went home. The next day we both went to work, and I informed everybody that I'd been married over the weekend. And that was it.

Well the first night I was terrified as to what was going to happen. I got into bed and he cuddled me. He said, 'Well, you've had a very busy day, you just go to sleep and what happens tomorrow will happen tomorrow.' Now that's what he said. He was very, very considerate. He knew I was tired and upset and that gives you an idea of what the man was like.

I'd never had any dealings with men, you know, and it was a bit of surprise. But I thought, 'Oh well, take it as it comes – it's something that happens and there you are.' We used to go out walking and he used to tell me all the things that had happened to him during the days and I told him all the things that had happened to me and I suppose we were great friends. For a long time I never knew where all the passionate love came in that I read about in all the books. I never found any of that, but we were companions and we were friends. We never, ever quarrelled about anything. We always asked each other whether that was all right and I suppose we were considerate of each other. I know he was to me. He was always very, very kind and very, very nice.

Edith with her husband Fred and three of their four children.

I didn't really have any expectations. I was thankful really for every day and every day was a kind of adventure because it had been such a stilted life I'd led, you know, being kept in as a child and never really being able to mix with anybody. To do all these wonderful things, like getting on a bike and riding somewhere where you hadn't been before was a joy. That I had to cook and clean was just another joy to me at that particular time. I enjoyed being married, because Fred wasn't demanding. He was always kind and helpful and never seemed to get cross with me. I suppose sometimes I did things that he didn't approve of but we never really had quarrels, never. So I suppose, you can call that love. I don't know.

I didn't really know whether he loved me or not. We got on well together. We agreed on most things. We laughed, and we read, and we walked. And we adored the children. He never told me he loved me, never. But he'd give me the top brick off the house. It was very − companionable, the whole time; it was better after I came alive and realised what life could be like. After about thirty I realised that women could enjoy the physical side of marriage, but it took me ten years to find out. Life improved tremendously then.

We were together sixty-two and a half years. So whether we loved each other at first, I never even thought about it. I must have been about thirty, and I was looking forward to going to bed with him, before I realised what people were talking about, which surprised me really. It kind of all slotted into place, but it took a long time for me to know what life was all about.

Edith and Fred had four children. They moved out of London to the suburbs in order to give the children a better environment in which to grow up. All their children have done well for themselves.

Unfortunately Edith died in November 1992, but up until her death she led a very active life: she walked her dog twice a day, attended aerobic classes, did all her own decorating, played bingo one night a week, babysat for her grandchildren and still found time for a daily game of scrabble with her close friend and neighbour, Percy. 'It's companionship that I think is nice.'

2 We Grinned and Beared It

When Kathleen Norton and Colin Thomson qualified as young doctors in the mid-1920s, Britain was on the edge of the longest economic depression so far this century. In the slums of London and the industrial North, each of them was fighting daily battles against poverty, disease, dirt and despair. Today they are still haunted by memories of their helplessness in the face of suffering, as children died of diphtheria and tuberculosis, and women fell sick, weakened by too many pregnancies. Before the advent of penicillin, antibiotics and effective inoculation programmes, these doctors had few weapons to combat the everyday killer diseases exacerbated by poverty. Nor had their patients the money to pay for the medical services which were needed. 'You've just got to do the best you can in rotten conditions,' says Kathleen Norton.

Many poorer families faced a choice between paying for the doctor or buying food. They might call the doctor for the man, if he was insured; or in extreme emergencies. Women and children especially lost out, suffering long untreated chronic illnesses. Typically families relied on home cures, quack remedies from the shops, or 'just sweating it out'. For the long-term sick, unable to work, the only recourse was often still the old workhouse hospital, as David Taylor recalls here his own slum childhood.

Perhaps the darkest side of medicine was the area of mental illness, which was surrounded by ignorance and secrecy. It was a time when a woman could be put away in a mental asylum for having an illegitimate baby. Charlotte Huggett's mother was committed to a mental asylum suffering from depression and remained there for fifty years until her death. So profoundly affected was Charlotte that she kept her mother's illness a secret all those years.

Cicely McCall, a pioneer psychiatric social worker, was among the few who were trying to change people's attitudes to the mentally ill. After helping to combat the evils of the White Slave Trade in Egypt, she attempted to humanise conditions in women's prisons and borstals. Her career eventually led her to specialise in mental health, where she saw the advent of such new drugs as Largactyl miraculously change the lives of some of her patients.

All five contributors recall their experiences in the days when the free health care of the National Health Service was still thirty years in the future.

KATHLEEN NORTON *was born in Kennington, London, in May 1899, into an old medical family: like her grandfather, her father was a G P, and her mother had trained as a nurse, although she never qualified. She had an elder sister, who in future years stayed at home to look after her parents, and three younger brothers.*

From the age of eight Kathleen wanted to be a doctor, but her father was opposed to the idea until he witnessed the competent role women played in the First World War. He relented and in 1918 allowed his daughter to go to St Hugh's College, Oxford, to read medicine as a pioneer woman student: 'There wasn't a medical book in the library.' While she was at Oxford she took part in various experimental medical research projects, such as the use of the first electro-cardiogram and studies of the effect of lack of oxygen on the body. After graduation, Kathleen went on to St Mary's Hospital, Paddington, following her father's path, and then when she qualified in 1925 she joined his practice in Kennington. When he died, slowly, of tuberculosis, she continued working from the same surgery.

My father was a very good general practitioner, a most caring one. I was thinking the other day, when I was about eight or nine, I came home from school and there was a strange child dressed in my best muslin Sunday frock. I thought, what's all this? The poor kid's mother had died of an overdose of cocaine in a back street – you see, one room and a gas stove on the landing. Father wasn't going to leave the poor kid there alone with a dead mother, and so he brought her to our house, and mother put her into my frock.

You see we lived on the job. My father did Sunday, and we didn't have a day off until I had a half-day in 1934. It was a vocation, not a money-making affair: at least in my time it certainly wasn't. Father and I didn't do it for the money. You do it for love of the job. And the patients: you care about them.

We charged two and sixpence. And we gave good drugs. Father wouldn't have anything from Boots, which was cheap in those days. So you had to work very hard for very little money. And you had private patients – but who were they? The clergy: and you don't charge the clergy. The surgery was an extension. It was very gloomy, done up with pine, dark brown, shiny; and had a gas fire in it, and a table in the middle with some books on. We had a dispensary on the ground floor and a dispensor who lived in the house. You had rhubarb and soda that you gave to nearly everybody, couldn't do any harm; cough medicines and iron and things like that for the children. Before I qualified, I used to go down in the evening and help, mix up the non-difficult medicines, the harmless ones; everything with morphia in or like that, the dispensor did. But I gradually learnt that way.

I had to buy the practice when my father died. You bought the practice at a year and a half's purchase money. I had to pay it over six years, and I had to pay interest on the rest of it. Before I retired, I took a partner.

When I qualified, it was difficult for me, because you see some of the patients had known me all my life. One of them said to me one day, 'I used to push you out in your pram, when you were a baby.' I got on better with the men. They were frightened of me. The reputation I had was, 'Don't go to 'er if you only want a certificate, but if you're really ill she'll struggle for you.' But you did have an awful time. All you could do was to help them with common sense. If you had pneumonia and you went round to see them, they'd have a huge fire in the bedroom, and they'd shut up all the windows and they'd even put cotton wool across the cracks. I would go in and say, 'You must have some air in this room,' and I would open the window. Then I'd go back two or three hours later down the same street, and find the window shut, and I would bang on the door and open the window again. It was a permanent battle for what I call common sense.

Kathleen, aged fifteen, with elder sister Phyllis and two of her brothers. From left to right: Phyllis, Alan, Kathleen, Geoffrey.

I was the 'parish doctor', which meant that if anybody hadn't got a doctor of their own, I had to attend. Even if she was a princess or a derelict, I had to go. I went into a basement one day and there was this poor woman lying in the middle of a large bed, and there were bits of horse-hair [from the mattress] on the floor, all around, everywhere, where the mice had been in. I had to bend over this poor woman and see what was the matter with her. I had to send her to hospital. I sent her bed away to be stoved, and they said, 'Do you want the bed back?' I said, 'It'll walk back. It's absolutely verminous, the whole thing.' It was terrible the way they lived.

Another one I went to see, she had what looked like a grey vest on. The neighbour who called for me said she had given the old lady a pink vest at Christmas, and this was somewhere in the summer, and it was grey. She had never had it off. And there she was, lying in filth; she'd had diarrhoea, poor dear, and nobody'd done anything for her at all. So I had to send her to hospital, and the poor nurses there had to bathe her and scrape off all this nonsense. I was so furious that they could be allowed to live like that and nobody know. But I don't know how anybody can know unless they've got relations to tell them.

I went to another basement and was let in by a poor little child of about twelve, clutching a small baby, in a long dress. We went into the basement front room and there was this woman lying in bed, and she'd been bleeding. There was another baby on a cushion in a chair. I was horrified and said, 'Why do you go on having these babies if you're miscarrying like this?' And she said, I've never forgotten it, she said, 'My husband likes me like his breakfast.' And I thought, 'Well, really!' He was a part-time waiter in Soho and he used to drink up all the remains of the bottles that the people left. Then he'd come home and he'd have his wife, like his breakfast. The poor wretched woman, she was miscarrying; you can't really blame her in a sense, on the other hand it is pretty awful. If you send her to hospital, what do you do with the twelve-year-old child and the two little babies? You've just got to do the best you can in rotten conditions.

Now pneumonia, you couldn't miss that if you were a doctor. You heard this extraordinary noise on the chest, quite odd. Nothing else makes a noise like that. They would have a temperature, probably 103 or 4, for about eight days, and then their temperature would come down with a run in a couple of hours. If you were there at the right time you could give them something like digitalis, which would keep their hearts going over the rapid descent of their temperature. Of course you never see that at all now; no modern students ever see it now.

And then there was rheumatic fever. That was awful, because it afflicted not the feckless patients, but the nice family that looked after their children but probably lived in slightly damp houses. And these children would get heart trouble; they would get an infection on the valve of their hearts. You had to put them flat in bed. And I would like to see them every day. But if you saw them every day you took more than their wages, so what did you do? Either you didn't see them every day, or else if you did, when the bill came in you doctored the bill. One family I remember, I think there were four children and three of them had this heart trouble, and they all worked in Woolworth's, standing on their feet all day. You couldn't persuade them to try and get a job where they sat down. In those days, you see, there was no operation for rheumatic fever. Nowadays they can operate on the valves.

But I'm not equipped for treating the mentally ill. I just am not. I like proper medicine, you know, things that I can see and handle and listen to and cope with. And I can't help thinking that those sort of people ought to be able to control themselves. I know they can't, my mind tells me they can't, but I still somehow feel that they ought. They're poor things, if you know what I mean. Now my brother, you see, is the other way on. He was a psychiatrist and he dealt with all those sort of people. But I found it very difficult.

I had to cope with them of course. I had one, whose family had shut him in because he had acute religious mania. He broke the window with a broom and got out, and went around to the church, and I was sent for in a hurry. Every time I appeared at the front of the church he ran around the back, and the rector and I chased him round the church, and we had a terrible job catching him. In the end he was found praying outside the front door, and we had to get the ambulance and keep him quiet and all the rest. But it takes years off your life if you have a case like that. And that same day afternoon, I had to take a cousin into Bethnal Hospital, to Croydon, in my car. She'd had a love affair in Germany and her family wouldn't let her marry the German. And she kept saying, 'Give me a tablet and let me die.' That was really the most terribly exhausting day!

And then in 1939 it was the war. Every time there was a siren, everybody rushed down the tube, next door to my house, as soon as the warning came. The lifts all stopped, so you had to run down eighty-two circular stairs to the bottom. I was supposed to pay a visit every night, to do an evening surgery, as it were, for people who couldn't get to their own doctors because the siren very often went at half past four or five, as soon as it got dark. So I had to go down and walk around the platforms and appear not to mind. They said, 'What's it like on top?' And I'd say, 'Oh, not bad,' when you'd just heard a huge bump and you were wondering if it was your house or not.

Then I had to crawl about in the ruins, and that was a scream because first they gave me a doctor's white coat which would have fitted a six-foot gentleman. I said, 'This is absolute nonsense.' So I went up to Marshall and Snelgrove and said, 'Can you build me a siren suit or something?' We had it made of velour cloth, like Navy overcoats, with zips in the sleeves so that I could pull them up, and a zip up the front, here, with lots of pockets. When I got it home I didn't like the long legs so I cut them off about halfway down so that I could feel more free to move about. I called them my 'bomb rompers'. That was invaluable if you were lying on your tummy with your face in a fireplace, and the patient on the other side. Very often I couldn't get back, so they used to take me by the legs and pull me back that way, because otherwise I couldn't have got out.

You're faced with perhaps just a black stocking and the rest of the patient isn't visible at all. All you want to know is whether they're alive or whether they're dead, and you can't tell if you've just got a leg like that, in a black stocking. So you inject it straight through the black stocking, and hope they were dead anyway and if they weren't you gave them a great dose of morphia which would help them out. I had a lot of that sort of thing to do. And I had to stand about in streets, stand and stand and stand, while the heavy rescue, as they were called, tried to get people out.

Originally there were no loos, no nothing, down the tube. What do you do with all those people down there half the night, when there's nothing for them? In the end they had Elsans and the shelter wardens had to take the Elsans up in the lift as soon as the raid was over and empty them down the drains on the top. Also, there were no bins for anybody to put sanitary towels or anything like that in. So I rang up the town hall and I said, 'Please can I have a dustbin for my people down the tube, because there's nowhere to put anything like a used sanitary towel.' They'd never thought of anything like that at all. I think I got the dustbins in the end because the medical officer who knew me said, 'Oh well, she'll nag away until you give her something, so you might as well do it straightaway.'

I wanted to have some cough medicine for the children, because a child coughing can keep fifteen hundred people awake. I couldn't have the cough medicine, wasn't on the schedule. So, of course, I went to my house and produced bottles of cough medicine from my own stock. I wasn't going to have the whole station kept awake all night long for something like that!

When you're living in an area like I was living in, a poor area, there was no beauty about anywhere, not in the back streets of Kennington. But when I was a student in Oxford I got into the Oxford Bach Choir. I've always sung all my life, and if you sing things like the B Minor Mass and the Matthew Passion it takes you out of this world. In the war, we did the Matthew Passion one year in the Albert Hall on practically no rehearsals. I used to say to God, 'Now for goodness sake just let me sing the Matthew Passion, then you can bomb me the next day if you like.'

There was a bomb in Hyde Park the day before the concert, and when we screamed 'Barabbas', as you do in the Passion – 'Barabbas!' – just like that, down came bits and pieces off the roof. They had to have wire netting strung across the top of the Albert Hall to stop it falling off. But it was marvellous just to be able to go and sing like that in the war, as though the war wasn't there. It took you right out of the conflict and all the things you'd seen and done.

Dr Kathleen Norton continued working in Kennington until 1962, when she retired. She now lives in a delightful cottage in Sandhurst, Kent, and is an excellent gardener. Kathleen never married, partly because 'I never met anyone from my class and background in Kennington'. Still passionately fond of singing, and having sung second soprano for the London Bach Choir for fifty years, she now sings alto for the Cranbrook Choral.

COLIN THOMSON *was born in Dublin in September 1900, but was brought up in the north-east of Scotland. He came from an army background: his father was a major in the Scottish Highlanders. 'In Scotland,' Dr Thomson says, 'the first son is supposed to be a parson, the second son a regimental general, and then, after that, medicine. So they wanted me to be a parson really, but I said to them that I would sooner be a doctor because I could minister to their bodies as well as their souls. I meant to be a doctor all the time I was young; it was a foregone conclusion.'*

He went to medical school in Edinburgh in 1917 and because he was a student he missed action in the First World War. When he qualified in 1922, he would have preferred to be a surgeon, but ended up as assistant to a G P in Rotherham, a poor industrial steel town in Yorkshire.

I had an appointment with the Poor Law Authority as a medical officer and the result was I had to look after the, well, lower third of humanity you might say.

In those days rickets was very common, particularly in the big cities – in Glasgow particularly, it was full of rickets. The typical rickety person had a big head – a head like a philosopher, a chest like a whippet, a belly like a poisoned pup and legs like a grand piano. That was the description of the ultimate in rickets. But of course we've no rickets any longer because people don't live in those terrible tenements any more. They never saw the light of day, and they never got proper food.

Rotherham – it grieved me. I used to see these poor children, and it was a thing that got me down quite a lot. But it didn't mean that I wanted to get out of medicine. I saw one child with a septic meningitis in its ear, and it was going to die, and I knew it was going to die. And I actually cried. Which is very foolish: you know you shouldn't do that sort of thing.

To tell you one of the most harrowing experiences, a woman came into the surgery one day with a little girl, in a blanket. When I pulled the blanket apart, there was the poor little mite, desperately ill. She was breathing very rapidly, and I had an idea what was wrong. When I looked in the child's mouth I was absolutely appalled, because the whole of the back of the throat, and the palate as well, was full of pus, and a dirty great white membrane was stuck across the whole of the back of the throat. And the poor child's neck was swollen right to the chin. Now, I knew what this was. The smell, which was characteristic of diphtheria, clinched the whole thing. She was so ill she couldn't cry. I had to send her to the fever hospital and the poor little mite – died – the same afternoon. Now, that's – a picture – of the sort of terrible disease – it should never be – it was the most harrowing thing I've ever had in my life. I'll never forget it.

Tuberculosis, particularly pulmonary tuberculosis, was another big killer. It used to come often in young people, adolescents, people in their early twenties. It was very common then. Now some got very ill and ultimately developed what was called a hectic fever. You recognised it. It presaged the end of the poor soul. The strange thing about these sick young people was that they developed a terrific optimism during this period. It was – pitiful to see it, because you knew they were going to die; yet they would have a superlative optimism. They would talk about what they were going to do, and where they were going and who they'll do it with and all this sort of thing. It was given a special name: it was called Spes Phthisica. Now *spes* is the Latin for hope and *phthisica* was the name of pulmonary tuberculosis in the olden days. Hence the name 'Spes Phthisica'. Ultimately, of course, tuberculosis was banished from this country with antibiotics. The sanitoria were all closed and gone. Unfortunately I believe it's coming back again.

I had a number of patients with syphilis. They were mostly businessmen. Everybody falls, and trips, don't they? Their wives didn't know. They were in the late stage, and they had the results. They drank a lot, they smoked cigars, and they didn't seem to bother. Syphilis is only infectious in the early stages when it's got the rash on it. Afterwards it's a different thing altogether. It can mimic any sort of disease, and we always had to keep it in the back of our minds in the 1920s.

In my fourth year at university – I hadn't qualified, I shouldn't have been – I was giving an anaesthetic to a patient who was in for an operation on that unmentionable thing, 'piles'. 'Haemorrhoids' to the aristocracy! His legs were trussed up and the surgeon was sitting in between the legs, gloved, ready to start. I could see him looking suspiciously at the site of the operation, and then with his gloved hands he started messing about. And all of a sudden he got up off his chair, tore off his gloves, threw them in the receptacle, which was in between the legs, and said (and these are not his words), 'Get this unrighteous man off the table, and take him to the pox department. He's got syphilis! These aren't piles at all, they're chancres!' That was my first experience of syphilis.

There were heaps of people who had heard so many shocking tales about operations done without anaesthetics that they had an absolute horror of surgery. They would say, 'I'd sooner die than face the knife.' That was the way they regarded it. They had all sorts of home cures of their own, you know. If a man cut his hand and bled very badly, he got some cobwebs off the wall or the roof and put it on; that stopped the bleeding. That's nature's way of doing it – with fibrin – which is just like a cobweb. They also used to let orange skin grow a mould and they used to put that on septic wounds. Now that was long before the days of penicillin, but there was probably penicillin in this mould.

But the worst part of the peripheral medicine were the quacks. A husband called me down, and he told me straight that his wife didn't like doctors but she'd had a man who said he specialised in this and that and the next thing, and had attended her for quite a long time. He'd decided that he'd done all he could and she should see a doctor.

Now these quacks, they were very clever; they knew exactly the time that they should disappear. So this man had disappeared and the husband had sent for me. When I saw the woman there was some sort of a plastering on the side of the face. Fortunately I managed to get it away and what I saw, honestly, it was hardly believable. She must have had what we call a rodent ulcer, but this fellow had been treating it with all these poultices, and the whole side of her face, the bone of the skull, was all eroded. It had gone. And her brain, you could see it pulsating in the huge gap of the wound. The big vessels of the neck, right down there, were exposed. I could do nothing for her. It was a case of just easing her passing, for as long as was necessary. We had morphia to deal with that. The husband was furious when I told him what the thing was like. He said, 'If ever I see that man I'll murder him.' And I'm sure he would have done.

I think we were very good at diagnosis. As far as a GP is concerned, most of the things he deals with and tries to treat, the recovery comes from nature, and the patient's resistance to disease. It had nothing whatever to do with medicine. We used to be able to treat – symptoms.

Colin graduated from medical school in Edinburgh in 1922. His parents would have liked him to become a parson but 'I meant to be a doctor all the time I was young; it was a foregone conclusion.'

For instance, if a patient has a cough, we had wonderful mixtures for coughs. And we always had something to ease terrible pain, like morphine. But the main thing was that ninety per cent of these ordinary diseases get better by themselves. The main thing about treating these illnesses was, just do as little as you can. Stand by and watch nature. You encouraged the patient and that was all you did. We called it 'masterful inactivity'.

I was a social worker. I simply did my job as well as I could. I always had a soft spot in my heart for women, particularly poor maiden ladies, who had very often a couple of aged relatives to look after for years and years. And they missed life, and everything connected with life. My philosophy? Well, I suppose it was Christian – but I wasn't. You remember *The Water Babies*, Miss Do-as-you-would-be-done-by? That was my philosophy.

Dr Colin Thomson left Yorkshire in 1933 and went to work as a GP in Pinner, a middle-class suburb of London. 'Oh the wonderful air, it was almost like Scotland where you come out of the train at Aviemore, marvellous. Air, straight from the gods – Olympus! And that is one of the reasons I decided on Pinner.'

Having retired in 1965, he and his wife still live only a short walk from his old surgery. As he says, 'I have always liked children and I think that children liked me' – and certainly his gentle bedside manner was one to be admired. To this day he can still be reduced to tears when he remembers the suffering of the sick children he treated in the slums of Rotherham.

But the people Dr Thomson left behind when he moved to Pinner had no hope of following. They continued to witness and suffer diseases bred of poverty.

•

DAVID TAYLOR *was born in 1898, the youngest of three, in the slums of Manchester, where his father worked in a local slaughterhouse. When he was small both his parents drank and both were violent, and the family slept on top of egg-boxes, all five in one room. Instead of a toilet they had to use a common earth closet in the yard.*

It really stunk. In them days you had no toilet rolls. We used to have the *Manchester Evening News* if you could afford it, that was a halfpenny, and you tore it up into little squares and put it on the hook and that was your toilet paper. We were really a rough lot – there was the gang that used to be called the 'bum smackers'. This was done during the day because you couldn't see a person's bum if it was dark. The bum smackers would go down quietly, moving the little door away and looking up to see if there was somebody on the midden; they might perhaps only find one or two from perhaps fifty houses on each side – but if they caught one they used to smack their bum and off they'd go. Some of them used to go round with tar on the end of a stick and put tar on the bum when they smacked. I was as bad as the rest of them. They couldn't catch us.

We were all lousy, every one of us. We'd have to use a small tooth-comb to get the lice out of us heads every day. We used to borrow the tray, after one had finished, put in on your knee and scrape your scalp with a small tooth-comb and the lice'd come out, you see. Poor old dad, I can see him now, when he was doing it, he'd be cracking 'em all down – we used to kill 'em all wi' our thumb as they come out of our head. We were all lousy, and yet we tried to keep clean. You could go out in the street and it was a common thing for to just take one off you and put your foot on it. It was thought nothing to have bugs, you know. And the wallpaper's there, if you peel it off you'd find it's infested with bugs, infested with 'em. So, although you had your bug bites they didn't seem to do you any harm. We all did it, see.

Scarlet fever and diphtheria were common. There was always the yellow van coming down from Monsal Fever Hospital carting them away. I think it was the hygiene conditions, why there was such a lot of diphtheria and the other ailments. And the death rate was very, very high with children.

It was a common saying that 'you're never a mother until you've lost one,' see. I should think that nearly every woman in those days lost one. They just had the ordinary rough midwife come to them, and she used to do the job, and if it wasn't done proper the mother died or the child died. My mother lost two but I think it was probably over-laying. When a child was born, you see, they had to put it somewhere, and of course it was a common thing to put it in the bed between man and wife. Perhaps the poor woman used to welcome the child in there to keep her husband from lusting after her, you see. Well, you see what happened. You only needed to pull the sheet over your head and the poor little child, it couldn't breathe. And they called it 'over-laying', overlie.

If you got sick, you used to lie on the sofa and perhaps have some lemonade; we used to think it helped us get better. We used to lie and work it off. Of course, if you got too sick you could go to the doctor, but you had no money to pay him. He would come around on a Friday night, have you down for how much you owed him, try and get his money back. There was the Hulme Dispensary on Stratford Road; you could get a bottle of medicine and perhaps a little bit of treatment there. But you didn't get anything for nothing – you had to pay for everything. There were no special services to help you out a bit, no health service or anything like that.

David was twenty-five and Glad twenty-two when they married in 1924. She still wears her twenty-three shilling wedding ring now 'paper thin'.

We used to be hungry and we'd go the soup kitchen, a gang of us, as soon as we came out of school. We used to line up, and on the other side would be Irish navvies that couldn't get work. They were really hungry. If you were out of work your family had to try and keep you some way or other. If you couldn't be kept you were put on Parish Relief. The Relief Officer used to come round and give you so much for your rent and so much for your food. It might be only about fifteen shillings. Well if the rent was, say, seven shillings – it was a struggle to keep the whole lot of you on. Every so often they

used to stop that and put the husband in the workhouse, more or less deliberately to penalise him, if he couldn't get work. They would send him in there for about six weeks.

When I married we had a lodger, Simmy, he had to go into the workhouse on task work every six weeks, task work, and then he would come out again. That was the only thing that existed if you were destitute. And nobody was allowed to wander about at night after twelve o'clock: you were liable to be questioned by the police. If you had no home and you hadn't got, I think it was one and six in your pocket, you could be arrested as a vagrant and a vagabond. That was the law them days.

There was hardship, we went through it. You submitted: we grinned and beared it. They sent them to the workhouse, they just accepted it: didn't use violence. They had unemployment meetings, but they were always quelled. We had fortitude, we stuck it really. I don't think there will be another generation like us, the Victorians.

David Taylor was called up as a young conscript in 1916 and worked in the engine-sheds. Much to his annoyance, he cannot remember Armistice Day at all as he was suffering from the Spanish flu, which is reputed to have killed more people than the many who died in the First World War. Fed up with looking for work in the postwar recession, he signed up with the Grenadier Guards – 'for a three-year stint with nine years reserve'. He met his future wife, Glad, who was a

parlour maid in Buckingham Palace Gate, when he was stationed at Chelsea Barracks. They had two daughters.

He left one army and joined another — the Salvation Army — and then worked as a postman until he retired at the age of sixty-three. David and Glad now live in Preston, where he enjoys bicycling. Even though a recent hip operation has hindered his mobility, he is planning a ten-mile sponsored tricycle ride for a new brain scanner for the local hospital.

•

CHARLOTTE HUGGETT *also came from a poor working-class family, but this time the poverty of the southern countryside, where even a regular farmworker's wage was not enough to sustain a family. Born in 1903, one of five children of whom only three survived, she grew up in the village of Wateringbury in Kent.*

My father was a farm labourer and we lived in a very small cottage. My mother went out to work as well as my father. We were very, very poor but very, very happy.

My brother died when he was three months old with whooping cough. I remember the little white coffin being up on the chest of drawers, and I think he used to sleep in a drawer because we had not got a cot for him. Then my other sister died of diphtheria at four years old, and I was in hospital with her at the same time. That was the only time in my life that I can remember sitting on my mother's knee, having these three injections on my back. I don't remember very much about it, I suppose I was too ill, but then I woke up and found my sister in the cot, by my side, so I was very pleased about that.

One night there was a lot of commotion going on and my little sister's cot was covered round with screens and the doctors and nurses were coming and going. In the morning when I woke up she wasn't there, so I asked where my sister was and they said that she had gone to Jesus and that quite soon I would see her again, when I went to Jesus. I thought that I was going to die, because I knew what that meant, and I got very panicky. For a few days I didn't know anything at all. I sort of saw people coming and going; then when I really came to, I saw my mother and father through a window. My bed was pushed up and I was able to talk to them. But I stayed there for about another two months. I went in at Christmas time and came out in the spring.

My father had heart trouble. Quite often he would have a heart attack. So we would go and get the brandy bottle and give him his brandy. But this one particular night, my mother was ill also – I think something went wrong with her brain, she was having one of her turns – so it was very necessary to go down and get the doctor. There were no cars, no bicycles. So with the storm lantern, my sister and I would start out to the doctor's, which was about three miles to walk. We would go down through these lonely woods, dark woods, no lights. We were always happy as long as we had our hands to hold, and the storm lantern; that gave you a lot of confidence. We never called the doctor out if only one of them were ill, but when they were both ill it was necessary.

My mother had these attacks when she wanted to 'do herself in'. We children knew about them, so we were sort of prepared for it. My sister and I would go downstairs at night when she had these turns and hide everything that was sharp. But we always had to get them out before she got up in the morning because by that time she would be her normal self and she would wonder where they were.

Why people didn't have the doctor very much was because they hadn't got the money. When the money was paid for the doctor, there was less for food. I can see my mother with her shabby purse now, putting the money in, taking the money out; whether I should go and get the eggs or not, because if we had the eggs there wouldn't be the money for the doctor. I can see her doing it now.

People made up their own mixtures and medicines. In the house when we had a cold, my mother would bake something that was called a wurzel, a vegetable that was given to the animals like a swede or turnip, that was cut up with brown sugar and baked in the oven, and the juice of that you had. When you had a very bad cold, they had beer in a glass, I suppose it was stout, and they put a poker in the fire, got it hot and – plunged it into the beer. Then they put ginger in it and you drank that. We didn't like it very much, but we thought it was a marvellous treat. Also every Friday night every child was given a dose of liquorice powder or Epsom salts. Every child had to have that on Friday because you were not going to school the next day or Sunday School. It wasn't drastic, it was just a thing to keep you 'clean' for the week.

It was decided, I think I was about eleven, that I should have my tonsils out. I was always having tonsillitis. So my mother made the appointment and we went to the hospital, which was free for the very poor. I was put in a room with I suppose about twelve or thirteen other children, most of them crying, and they had great difficulty in getting each child to go into the next room. When I got in and saw they had a big bowl of tonsils there, all heaped up in a kidney bowl, I said to myself, 'Well, I won't open my mouth.' But you sat on the nurse's lap and she put her legs round your legs and held your face hard. I started to cry, she said, 'That's good, that's good.' Then they swabbed your throat with something and they just snipped it off. You could feel that something was happening although not actual pain. Then you went into another room with all the children who had had theirs done, just spitting blood into a bowl.

After that I walked five and a half miles back home. My father was cross because I had the nurse's bruises on my face for about a week, where her hands had held me. The next time I had them out (they grew again because they only sliced them), I was in hospital for a week. I was put to sleep and knew nothing about it!

My elder brother died at fourteen with meningitis; he was in an orphanage by that time. Before my brother died, my father died, when I was thirteen. My mother went into a mental hospital about one year later, and then my brother died soon after. So at fourteen, and my sister was sixteen, we were left homeless. We were both homeless for ten years, until my sister got married and made a home. But it didn't worry us very much because we were in domestic. I was training to be a nanny and my sister was in the kitchen. It's when you get older that you realise that you miss your mother and father, but not as children because you are too busy working.

I was away working when the lady [of the house] came to tell me that my mother had gone away and she was in hospital. The uncle who put her in, that was her brother, found her down by the river – she was going to put herself in the river. My uncle said, 'You've had three attempts, and now you go there and you stop there.' Which she did, for nearly fifty years all but ten months. It was very disturbing when we went to see her and she didn't know us. And it was very disturbing when she did know us. But gradually the pity overwhelmed everything and I used to go up regularly.

It was a big hospital, very, very big. They had their own farm, their own chapel. Thousands up there, strange people walking about, talking, as you go through the wards. You felt quite nervous when people put you through a locked door, and all these people talking strange things, and then you go through another door and another door. The worst ward of all was where there were children, even small children there. I think the dreadful part was seeing all the things that happened there, seeing people being put into straight-jackets, seeing all that sort of thing. It

Above: Wateringbury, Kent, 1907. Charlotte, aged four, is on the far left of the front row with elder sister Dolly next to her. Her baby brother Bob is sitting on their Grandmother's knee with Charlotte's mother, Annie Maria, behind.
Opposite: Charlotte, centre, as an under-nanny at a tea party in 1921.

made me feel perhaps that that would happen to me one day. So that dread was on your mind. Also, there was no one to talk to. My sister didn't understand; she just thought it was nonsense to worry, it never worried her at all, ever. She was able to have a boyfriend and tell him all about it and took him up to visit mother, and it didn't worry her. She couldn't understand why it should worry me.

When I had measles, I was taken into hospital and put into a children's ward because there was nowhere to put an adult with measles. When I woke up at night I saw these rows of cots and I saw white figures coming down like the Ku Klux Klan. Afterwards I understood: the people who came to visit their children had these white gowns on. Unfortunately, at the bottom of my bed, there was a Mongol child. I thought, 'At last, they have really put me in a mental hospital now.' And I picked up the board beside my bed and it said 'Metropolitan Asylum Board'. I got very panicky and shrieked, 'Where am I?', and I didn't get any satisfaction until there was a girl of about sixteen explained it all to me.

When I was a nanny, one day I was in the airing cupboard; there

had been a disturbance in the nursery. I was supposed to be having my rest but the second nurse decided she didn't want to take the children out alone, and I sort of rather rebelled. The small child was crying and when the mother came along, she said, 'What's the matter?', and the child said, 'Lottie doesn't want to come out with us this afternoon.' So later on in the day the housekeeper and the lady were talking outside the airing cupboard where I was sorting linen, and I heard the housekeeper say, 'She'll end up where her mother is.' As soon as they were gone, I went upstairs and packed my case; I was just going to run away, I don't know where. I came downstairs with my suitcase, but I was found. My sister was called and the lady talked to us both and in the end sent us out on a treat, in the car. The lady was very understanding and she talked things over.

When my mother went, I had nightmares and sleepwalking, because I felt they were putting me in. One of these nightmares the airing cupboard came into, only the door was shut and it was getting warmer and warmer. I went to my doctor and we talked for weeks and weeks, and at the end he said, 'Now, you'll never have another nightmare, and you'll never sleepwalk again.' And I never have. But the extraordinary thing, I didn't do any sleepwalking when I was looking after children, never once. I always knew when I had been sleepwalking because I'd come down in the morning and all the clocks would be altered, the doors would be open and the lights would be on. That's how I knew, but I never went outside the door because my bedsocks were never dirty.

When my mother died the doctor had me up at his house to help him look after his wife, who had had an operation, because he thought that I might have a breakdown. I think his attitude was one of the things that helped me. Now, if anybody has mental trouble they just say 'They're having a breakdown', and that sounds much nicer than being put into a mental hospital.

I felt very much better when the war came and they named the asylum 'Oakwood Hospital'. Also, there weren't so many locked doors. My mother was in a ward there you only had to go through one locked door. Otherwise you went through the padded cells where they put people who would do themselves in. I don't think my mother ever went into the padded cells.

With age she got better. She still would have made an attempt, but I think less. We had her out for four days at a time and she even came up to this cottage twice. People outside didn't know there was anything wrong with her at all; she was alright to talk to, very sensible and very happy to be out, but on the last day she was always packed and ready to go back.

It's funny, I always knew in my mind I wanted a house of my own, and that's why I collected my bottom drawer. Not for marriage, I never thought about a husband or a boyfriend, that didn't interest me at all. When I had boyfriends I never let it get serious because of my mother – because I would have to tell them. But my sister didn't mind; her boyfriend knew from the word go. But I never did, so I always kept them at bay. I knew if I married and had children that the madness might happen to them, and so I was very, very lucky that I've looked after all my other children and they have meant very much more to me because of that.

Charlotte looked after a total of twenty-one children while working as a nanny, and she never did marry. Even her married sister decided not to have children in case her mother's illness was found to be hereditary. Charlotte lives on her own in a cottage she bought many years ago and still keeps in touch with many of her 'children'. They are now parents themselves, and she helps out with babysitting and sewing on school name-tapes. 'I've always loved children.'

Coincidentally, 'Nanny' Huggett remembers meeting Cicely McCall, our next contributor, when the family she was working for took her on their travels to Egypt. But the two women came from widely different backgrounds.

CICELY McCALL *was born in London in 1899 and came from a privileged upper-middle-class professional background with servants and a governess for the children. Her father was a well-to-do K C and the family lived in comfort in Kensington, London, with a country house in Kent. It was a close and happy family, but by the First World War, their fortunes had changed. Her father lost most of his money and one of her brothers was killed in action. 'None of my friends earned their living and it never occurred to me that I should have to earn mine. I thought you lived a life of leisure. So it was quite a big shock.'*

Cicely went to Oxford University, paid for by her brother-in-law, and was sent down for a term for flouting a petty regulation. Disillusioned with education, she worked at various jobs, including being a mannequin and a saleswoman, then eventually trained as a secretary. She was twenty-seven when she applied for a job advertised in a newspaper to work in Egypt for an organisation called the 'International Bureau for Suppression of Traffic in Women and Children' – otherwise known as the White Slave Trade.

They said they wanted an organising secretary who could speak French and had some knowledge of committee work. I had no knowledge of committee work, but I could speak French and so I applied, and to my great surprise I was appointed. I trained for about two or three months in the London office and then I was sent out there. This was in 1927, and the police there were extremely helpful to me and took me to see the brothels and the red light district.

We had this hostel where we had girls who wanted to give up being prostitutes and find another job, and we housed them until they did find another job – which was very difficult, because there weren't really any jobs for women at all. If they were Europeans, they were generally sent back to their country of origin, which was often France, sometimes Italy, sometimes Greece. And if they were under-age they were deported. I only found one girl a satisfactory job, and she was quite an elderly French prostitute. She'd been brought up in a convent so she was a beautiful needlewoman and she went as a sewing maid to the British Hospital, where she ended her days. I suppose she was then about fifty but looked about a hundred.

I didn't quite believe the White Slave Trade existed like that, but all the horror stories you were told as a little girl were in fact true. You had French girls who were sent over in the Messagerie Maritime Steamships, and they were concealed in stokers' cabins, or sometimes in wooden cases. One girl said she was in a pipe – I suppose it was a very large pipe – but she was there for two days without any food. Sometimes they were sent there with the promise of a job which didn't exist, but a lot of pressure was used. When they got there, if they said, well, 'We don't care for this, we want to go home,' the man who'd been responsible said, 'Well you haven't got a passport, your passport is false, and if you declare yourself to the police you'll be put in prison.' So they had very little alternative. But if they heard about us, then they did come and ask for our help. Otherwise, there they were in the brothel under the supervision of the Madame. They didn't have any money, they had to work all the hours there were, and all they had was pocket money and their clothes. It was slavery.

I wrote a report for the League of Nations about conditions in Cairo.

I wrote about how people were forcibly sent to Egypt, how they were beaten and had no money, and I wrote about the incidence of venereal disease, which was very, very high in spite of all these regulations and examinations and so on, and how it was a degrading system. It got very good reviews – it was translated into various languages – and on the strength of that when I got home I was given a scholarship, which was called an American Commonwealth Scholarship, to go to the London School of Economics for a new course in mental health. This was in 1933 and it had only just started. We trained as psychiatric social workers, a year's training at the Maudsley Hospital and the London School of Economics. We were the first, and from there I could go on and work in mental hospitals.

But in fact I was offered a job in the prison service, Assistant House Mistress at Holloway and also at the girls' borstal in Aylesbury. I taught, I did quite a lot of library work, and made contact with the women. I was allowed to see all the case papers at Holloway, but at Aylesbury for some unknown reason I wasn't, which was very stupid because I was, after all, a trained psychiatric social worker. I think most of them were in for theft. They generally did about three years, and it was pretty primitive and restrictive. The governor was very much against any close association between girls – she always suspected the worst! She was against any make-up as a matter of course, which wasn't allowed anyway. But the girls always wanted to have some kind of make-up, so they would lick the cover of a red library book in order to get a little lipstick; they would use boracic powder, or flour if they could get hold of it, as powder. It was such a silly childish thing to do really, but they did it because of their frustration. For that they would have quite severe punishments, like putting back their date of discharge.

If they broke other rules, that is if they had made a noise in their cells or if they had been late for something, any stupid thing, they were made to crush bones in a pestle and mortar. A huge pestle and mortar. Each girl was in a separate cell with an open side to it which had bars, and the governor passed by this row of cells, one girl in each cell, each with a large pestle and mortar crushing bones which were used as manure in the garden afterwards. I can't remember how many hours a day they did this, but one of the prison rules was that the governor had to see every inmate once a day, every day. So she just said, 'Hello, good morning Mary, how are you doing?' and then passed on, and that satisfied that rule. But there was this girl, doing something totally unconstructive!

Later Cicely was able to introduce some reforms herself as head of an approved school for girls at Exeter.

I put them into normal clothes instead of the really awful uniform they had when I came. I took them on camp, which they loved. They learned housework and cooking and laundry. The same girls did gardening and I put the girls who did gardening into trousers and they thought this was the most exciting thing in the world. I found an old book in a cupboard which was, I suppose, about fifty years old, giving the punishments girls received if they did something wrong, or 'being rude to Matron'. You had your hair cut off, or you were shut in a little cell, where the gardener used to keep his spades, which was just long enough for a child to lie down in. It had a wooden door with a padlock on it and apparently they put the children in there. When I first came there they all called me Matron or Mum – 'Please 'um.' They'd say, 'Good morning, please 'um.' 'Yes, 'um, thank you, please 'um.' And I'd say, '"Please 'um's" not my name – my name's Miss McCall.' But they couldn't bring themselves to say that and it took months before I could get them to use my name.

After that Cicely was for seven years education organiser for the Women's Institutes, until she was sacked for standing as a Labour parliamentary candidate in 1945.

Cicely in 1937 before she published her first book They Always Come Back *about women offenders.*

So then I decided I'd better do what I'd been trained to do. It was the beginning of the National Health Service and I got appointed as Psychiatric Social Worker to a mental hospital in Suffolk, which was very exciting because they'd never had a social worker before, ever. It was a 1000-bed hospital and they had three medical staff and no social worker at all, and fairly limited nursing staff. The first medical superintendent when I was there played golf every afternoon, so he was never there after twelve o'clock and there were two other medical officers for the 1000 beds. One of them drank a good deal so he was generally out of it, and the other one worked all the hours that are and kept the hospital going. But with the introduction of NHS they got better medical staff and even got a canteen so that visiting relatives could have at least a cup of tea. Some of them had to travel twenty, thirty, forty miles to see their wife, or husband, and before that there'd been no way of them getting any cup of tea, or meal, or anything.

Towards the end of the time I was working in mental hospitals these wonder drugs came in like Largactil, which made an enormous difference, I mean, really a miracle. I remember one woman who had been in hospital quite a long time; she had been in Malaysia in the war and she was always just one step ahead of the Japs. She walked across the country carrying her baby with her, managed to get on to a boat and it took her to Australia, and there she was until the end of the war. Her husband was in the army and when they joined up again she had a very severe breakdown, I think entirely as a result of the lack of food and the really awful privation she'd gone through. Finally her husband couldn't cope any more and he got a separation and left her. He'd found somebody else. And I remember seeing her walk around the exercise yard in the hospital with stockings round her ankles, in hospital clothes. She used to draw the most terrible pictures of crucifixions with lots of nails sticking out of the bodies, and she was quite, quite insane. There seemed to be no hope for her at all. And then Largactil was discovered and she was given it. She recovered, she became self-respecting, she wore proper clothes, and she was finally discharged and became secretary of the local Women's British Legion in her village. She helped me with a flag day to raise money for the Norfolk and Norwich Association for Mental Health and I remember she said quite naturally, 'Oh I mustn't forget my Largactil – I must take it with my sandwiches.' And she did – she had no embarrassment about it and she was once more a self-respecting person, and it was all due to these marvellous drugs. They were a miracle!

When I'd retired I thought I was going to lead a life of leisure, but I was then asked to start a working group for the National Association for Mental Health in Norfolk. Ten of us sat together in my sitting room, we each paid half a crown for postage, and on those ten half-crowns we started an organisation which now gets subsidies in the region of hundreds of thousands of pounds. First of all we had lectures to tell people what mental illness meant and what the treatment was and what was being done for the mentally ill. I felt it was essential to tell a wider public what mental illness meant and that it was very often curable, and that they should understand it and not be afraid of it. I remember once we arranged transport for some of the mental patients who were in-patients to go and see their families. Volunteer drivers would drive them to their families because Norfolk's a very big place and they weren't always able to visit them. And one person said, 'Is mental illness infectious? Shall I get anything if I have her sitting beside me in the car?' Well that sort of ignorance amongst educated, normal people, let's face it, is quite staggering. But I think it was widespread then. They really thought that they could catch something from a schizophrenic. I don't think anybody thinks that now, but they did then.

A few years after that we started group homes for people who had been in hospital a very long time and had lost touch with their families or their families didn't want them, and they had no place to go. And I think running the group homes was probably the most exciting social work I'd ever done. We started with four elderly ladies and between them they'd been over a hundred years in a mental hospital. One of them had been in more than half her life. She was said to be a schizophrenic but I don't know really whether she was. One was a depressive, one had had an illegitimate child and in those days very often you were popped in a mental hospital for that.

We bought, on a loan, a house in Norwich, in a little side street, and there was a shop and post office nearby. I went over to them and said, 'Look, these people have been in hospital twenty, thirty years, in one case forty years. They won't know a thing. They don't know how to use the telephone, they won't know about change, they won't know about the prices. Can you help?' And the shopkeepers were marvellous. They said, 'Oh yes, our old Uncle Robert, he's in a mental hospital, we know all about that and we'll certainly help them.' And they did. It was quite contrary to our worst expectations.

When the ladies came to us they were like people coming from a desert island. They knew nothing about modern foods, I mean frozen peas were a revelation to them. They couldn't remember how long it took to boil potatoes; I mean, was it a minute or was it an hour? They just couldn't remember. So they did everything wrong, and yet somehow they persisted, because they were so anxious to have their freedom and run their own show. One of them was appointed housekeeper and everybody paid so much to her. They all drew their own pensions, whereas in hospital all they'd had was 'tuppence ha'penny' out of their pension every week – got all of their own pension, and it was a miracle to them.

And they cooked. They cooked in turn, even though they made every possible mistake. You know, they burnt the potatoes, they used the Hoover with the wrong end, they applied a match to the lamp as if it was on the gas. They didn't know what things cost; one went out and bought a sewing machine at the market and she didn't notice it hadn't got a needle, and of course, it was so old you couldn't get a needle for it – so it was a dead loss. Another bought a bicycle and it just fell apart with her on top of it. But they recovered and they went on persisting, and then gradually one or two of them left and got lodgings for themselves. It was certainly the most rewarding thing I did. And when I got an MBE for it, it was an MBE of course for the women. It was them that really deserved it; and it was them, they'd made a success of it.

Not content with setting up group homes for people who had been in psychiatric hospitals, Cicely McCall, at the age of seventy-eight, launched a charity called Operation Arthritis. Its aim was to raise money to build a new ward and operating theatre for the local hospital, in order to help more people have hip and knee replacement operations. She too has had her hip replaced, and was walking again in ten days and driving within six weeks.

Cicely lives in her own house near Norwich with a beautifully tended garden. She has an active social life and many friends.

3 The Demon in the Glass

Alcohol was the most popular means of escape from everyday life for men, and for many women too in Edwardian Britain: a path to temporary oblivion for rich and poor alike. As much as a sixth of all working-class income was spent on drink, mainly beer, and an average of six pints of beer a week was consumed for every adult in the population. Drunkards were commonplace, with many pubs open all day, and altogether one public house for every three hundred people. The police brought over 4500 prosecutions for drunkenness every week in London alone.

For working-class men, the pub was often the heart of a community, providing a refuge from often overcrowded living conditions and a welcome alternative to hanging about on street corners. They could congregate in its warmth and talk, smoke, sing round the piano, play simple games, as well as to drink. The pub took the place filled now by television, bingo or the cinema. As Harry Gillham says, 'There were no club rooms, no village hall, nothing like that. In those days if they wanted enjoyment, they had to go to the pub.' There was less space for women, even in pubs in the south, and elsewhere they were barely tolerated: in Jennie Armstrong's words, 'It was taboo for a woman to go in a pub. It was considered a terrible thing.'

The comfort and company men could find in a public house were the lighter side of the picture. The dark side was that drink was one principal source of poverty and violence in the home. The Temperance Movement fought back, seducing the young Edwardian male from the conviviality of the saloon bar with the flicker of magic lantern shows proclaiming the evils of alcohol. People 'signed the pledge' of abstinence in their thousands and the Band of Hope flourished, offering a rare place of respectable entertainment outside the home.

ALCOHOL: A FOE

A POISON, NOT A FOOD
LESSENS MUSCULAR MENTAL MORAL POWER
CREATES CRAVING FOR MORE
OBSTRUCTS GROWTH, UNLIKE MILK OR COCOA
HINDERS DIGESTION, HARDENS FOOD
OVERWORKS HEART, DOES NOT WARM
LEADS TO DISEASE, SHORTENS LIFE

A typical magic lantern slide, shown at Band of Hope meetings, depicting the 'evils of alcohol'.

One of the earliest casualties of the First World War was all-hours' drinking: licensing laws were introduced to regulate pub opening times. As Lord Soper says, 'War can only be efficiently carried on if you've got sober people to do it.' Between 1910 and

1930, alcohol consumption halved, a trend that continued into the 1950s, and its decline marked a critical social change: as alcohol consumption decreased, so did acts of personal violence. During that period Britain was probably a safer place to live, the Blitz excepted, than at any time before or since. From the 1960s onwards, there has been a rise in alcohol consumption which has been closely linked with a similar rise in violence.

This chapter takes us back to a time before licensing laws, when farms brewed their own cider, when pubs had no fixed hours and when men did not go home until all the money was drunk. Each of our five contributors recounts how drink, at some time in their life, for some reason or another, played an all-important role.

HARRY GILLHAM *was born in Bradford Abbas, in Dorset, in 1901, the only boy of five children. His father, a farm labourer, was blinded in an accident, leaving his mother as the sole provider: she had a cleaning job at the school as well as working in the laundry from four in the morning until ten at night. Although life was hard, Harry fondly remembers the good times he had drinking at the Rose and Crown or out in the fields with his friends.*

When I was nine years old I used to go to Yeovil to get the fish in a little hand cart, come back and be in school by nine o'clock. Out again at ten o'clock, go into the village with father to sell the fish. In school again at two, out at three or three-thirty, and perhaps go to Sherborne with the fish or up round new buildings. And when I finished my round I used to come back down Bradford Abbas about nine o'clock at night. I used to go in the pub and have half a pint. Father would have a pint of cider. It was threepence for ale, tuppence for beer. And I used to enjoy it. Children were going to pubs, that time then. They didn't care who drunk beer or whatnot. Children could always have a sip of beer if they wanted to.

If you went in the other room you could play darts, or six or eight or ten could sit down at the table and have a game of tippet. You put twenty-one strokes on the table – chalk strokes. Whoever won the toss for to hold the coin, you put all ten hands up on the table and the others, like, had to guess which hand it's in. They'd say, 'Take he away, take he away, take so-and-so away,' and as you'd win you'd cross out a stroke. You don't see none of those strokes today. 'Tippet' that was called.

We had skittles, see skittles, rings, darts, yes! Rings used to be a hell of a game. You had a board with hooks on it and then you had rubber rings. You used to fling them up and try to put them on the hooks. And

Harry, far right, as a young boy with his mother and sisters taken outside the laundry at Bradford Abbas, Dorset, where his mother worked.

of course, later on the cards come on, see, and we would play that. Every Saturday night if you weren't down the pub by half past six you couldn't get in. Because there was about eight high waiting to play and first come first served. You had to wait till they played the game right through and then you were allowed to take on the winners. The losers finished. We played for a sixpence.

See, they never had nowhere else to go. There was no club rooms, no village hall, nothing like that in those days, so if they wanted enjoyment they had to go to the pub.

Once we were working out at Manor Farm, there was thirteen of us. We used to do piece-work. I used to get on my push bike and goes to Compton with a five-quart jar and bring it back full of cider. And we sit up in the field where we supposed to be working, hoeing, and not hit a stroke. Only eat your food and drink your cider. You had your week's wages just the same because you're on piece-work. The farmer would come round and say, 'You want to get on with it', but we had a week of that straight off. But nobody used to get drunk though.

There was a farmer out here, he used to have a farm in Winchester. They used to make the cider down there and bring it from Winchester up here. But then you couldn't drink that because it was like vinegar. I went to the farm cellar one morning, four o'clock, when we were cutting seed for fodder. I filled the jar up, in the cellar – couldn't drink it, it was

bitter. Yet, when we was youngsters, we used to go apple picking down Winchester and we used to drink the new cider and that was lovely.

We used to grow a lot of parsnips and mother used to make the wine. We used to go and get the parsnips; mother used to wash and clean 'em, cook and boil them. Then put them in the barrel out in the coal-house shed, a four-and-half-gallon barrel, not a small one mind. Father used to go out to the tap and draw what he wanted. Draw out a bottle-full and carry it around in his pocket, like a whisky bottle. He used to drink that, take it down the pub and drink it with three pints of cider – and walk home. You could take a shilling down of a night time, have three pints of cider, an ounce of baccy and a box of matches and still have a halfpenny change. Yes, those days have gone now.

Harry never left Bradford Abbas. Like his father, he worked as a farm labourer, then, when work on the land became scarce, he found employment first in a bakery and later on the railways. He is now a widower, living on his own. He likes a bet and he keeps a large vegetable garden. He still enjoys a pint down at his local the Rose and Crown.

•

JENNIE ARMSTRONG *was a twelve-year-old pulling pints in her mother's dockside pub in Workington while Harry was enjoying his beer as a child in Dorset. Born in 1902, Jennie was four when her father died. Her mother remarried and Jennie was fond of her step-father but he became a 'war wreck', severely handicapped by shell-shock. So Jennie's mother ran a series of pubs single-handed.*

Now, you're not allowed to go behind the bar until you're a certain age, but in those days you had to go and help your mum. Right along the foot of the counter was about a six-inch trough full of sawdust and that was where the men had to spit. Why men spit, and they did that in those days, I don't know, but wherever they were, they used to spit. There was spittoons – round iron things – here, there and everywhere, for men to spit in, filled with sawdust, and that was awful. You'd empty that out and then black-lead it, with brushes and black-lead, and polish them up. My mother was awful particular about them. But that trough along the edge of the bar, that was terrible.

The urinals was worse. We had two: there was one in the back yard and then there was one on the outside of the house, and they were tarred, so far up, tarred, with a gunnel run down like that. Well, there was no running water: the human water used to run down the wall and along the gunnel. There was no chain or receptacle or anything like that. It

was just up against the wall. And every morning I had to go out there with the scrubbing brush and scrub all of this down. That was horrible as well, but that was one of the things you had to do.

The last pub we were in was the Ship Launch, and that was mainly sailors off the boats, plus the dockers, stevedores and what have you. If you got the officers in off the boats, they stuck with you, but if you didn't

Jennie at five years old sitting on her grandmother's lap in the garden of her mother's first pub, the Collier's Arms, in Camerton, Cumbria. Her mother Mercia is behind her and her brother Walter is at her feet.

get them to come into your pub you didn't do any business till another boat come in.

You stood outside – I was only maybe ten or eleven – looking as nice as you could, with a sweet smile on your face if they were passing that way. They had to pass the doors, and of course fellows that had been to sea for a long time would talk to you and pop in for a drink. You'd got them then, they were your customers.

We used to encourage them in lots of ways. My mother used to make sandwiches and then on the counter there was pipes, clay pipes, and you got one of those free if you were a smoker. And she had an urn on the counter with a bit of gas jet under it, and she would make Bovril. The workers would come in off shift, twelve-hour shifts six days a week, and they would have a cup of Bovril before they had a pint. But some of them could take their pints for ever more.

If we'd got them in when they got paid on the Friday, they would stay there until they'd spent up, and then the poor wives didn't get any money. Some of the wives used to come round and stand at the bar door, and wait, try and catch their men for a couple of shillings to go to the market to buy something for the kids. It was really hard times.

The woman used to get bashed when the husband went home at night. His dinner would be there, and of course waiting hours for his dinner, it wouldn't be fit to eat. He used to pick it up and throw it on the fire, and he would throw her out on the street, and he'd throw the kids out as well. This happened loads and loads of times. It was alright in the summer time but in the winter, poor, poor souls, it was dreadful. It was a case of, 'Look what our Tommy did last night to me,' and then there'd be a black eye, and a marked face. Oh that was regular, that was really regular.

My mother was nearly twenty stone, and was fit, really fit. She was a big woman, and she ruled with a rod of iron. Anybody started getting funny, which they did, she would just lift the lett – that was part of the counter – and just go through and take hold of them and say 'Out'. But nobody ever turned on my mother; they were great big fellows, and nobody ever turned on her that I can ever remember. She ruled her pub, she was the boss. So now you know where I get it from.

There was fights, but they would go outside to fight. They wouldn't wreck your bar. But I remember as a child out playing, and first one and then another come out. 'Oh come on, let's go on the shore, there's going to be a fight.' A couple of fellows would walk down to the shore and fight and walk back and have a drink together. Us kids used to stand all round and watch them, cheer the one we liked best.

I had to play the piano at ten years old while fellows were singing. They used to sing all them stupid songs, 'No-one Like Mother To Me', 'Don't Go Down the Mine Daddy', you know. Everybody would be crying – the more drink they got, the more sorrowful they felt. Oh dear! 'Six Feet of Earth Make You All of One Size' – I can remember the titles of all those songs but I couldn't tell you how they went. It was terrible, terrible! There were tears dripping in the pints and I would be vamping away on the piano. I couldn't play the tunes, I just used to vamp them – make a noise – it satisfied them, and they're supposed to go home feeling great, having a good night out.

But there was nothing, you see, in those days to what you have now. We had no telephones, we had no wirelesses or no televisions; there was nothing else to do. Men would play toss-penny; they would go in a group and toss a penny, and if it went in this ring they'd marked, well they won. Simple little games like that. And throwing a ball into a pint pot edged against the wall, tipped up a little bit, and if you could throw this little marble in this pint pot, you'd won. They were so very, very simple because there was nothing else to do. Then, if they had no money and they couldn't get a pint, of course tempers used to rise, and it was a back-hander if she got in the way.

I never saw any women sticking up for themselves. Never, ever.

There would be fights but no woman ever stuck up for theirselves. They were just like slaves, unless you were a little bit better educated. But so often it happened; you get hold of a nice young man, and once he was married he just used to turn. I'm not going against men. Don't think that, because I had a good husband, I had a good father, I had a good stepfather as well. But it was just something he had to do to make him look a man, to make him look as though he was somebody.

It was taboo for a woman to go in a pub. It was considered a terrible thing. We had a spot at the end of the bar called the jug and bottle. It was a little alcove with a shutter, and you used to open this shutter, it's no more than a foot square, and maybe women would come in, with a shawl on, with a bottle or a jug for a pint of ale and porter. As I got older I remember three ladies used to come in, and they'd be there with their shawls on and that little lett used to'open – 'Give us two penneth' – two pence for a small whisky, or small gin. Mind you, a lot of them used to buy that gin and give it to the kids, the babies, to put them to sleep. But they didn't go to sleep, and daddy comes back and hears them crying – and it was bang, bang, bang again.

You could open all day, because if you didn't you were losing money; they went somewhere else. My mother used to get up at six o'clock in the morning when the workers were building the pier, and they would all call for a pint on the way to work. But when it come to war days, they were making a bit more money; munitions shops and the steel works was going on and soldiers were coming on leave – there was more money about.

The licensing laws? Yes, yes, that was during the war. Then of course as the time went on, they started to ration your beer: they couldn't afford the time to make the beer, and you'd maybe get two barrels a week. So the pubs used to take it in turns to open. The steel works employed a lot of men, and they were coming off shifts at ten o'clock. Well you were supposed to close at ten o'clock, and you were up in court if you served a drink after that. So they all went in revolt. They were striking on the works because they couldn't get this pint when they finished shift. So they altered it to half past ten, and this area was the only area in the country that had a licensing law to half past ten. Everywhere else they had to close at ten o'clock.

It changed this way: you did a lot of sneaking. You served drink out of hours. You were breaking the law, and you were watching all the time, looking through your windows and such like. You were careful who you served drink to after time, in case they shopped you. The police was on the job and you never knew when they were going to pop round the corner. But they did serve drink, they didn't keep to the hours, not by any means, none of the pubs kept hours.

Jennie met her first husband in her mother's pub. He was a Scots sailor, 'tall, dark and handsome'. They had three children. She had one ambition:

I would have given anything to have had a pub of my own, anything. But my first husband, he liked his drink, being a sailor I suppose it's natural, and so there was no chance. My mother advised me, it would be a bad thing to do to take a pub with him liking it so much. And that's why I didn't, because I couldn't trust my husband, for if he couldn't get it there he would get it somewhere else. There was too many risks.

She spent a lifetime serving behind other people's bars and was working when, aged seventy-six, she met Bill, a shy bachelor over twenty years younger than her, who was a regular at the Commercial. They lived together for ten years before getting married eight years ago: 'a good man. I know with my experience, he's a good man.'

DONALD SOPER *who was born in 1903, grew up in a very different environment. His father worked in insurance and the teachings of the Methodist church inspired his family's life. They 'thoroughly enjoyed' music, singing to the piano and fiddle. But drink they were convinced was evil.*

As a child my life was a mixture of a close-knit family at home and an equally close-knit religious environment in the church, of which my father was an officer and a Sunday School superintendent. My mother was a teacher. It was the Methodist church in Wandsworth and I grew up in an atmosphere in which those two elements were so closely joined it never struck me that there was any difference between them. Church was as natural as sleeping in your own bed. I can't remember doing anything very much outside the peripheries of the home and the church.

I was persuaded that the nature of the good life was abstention from such evils as alcohol and betting and, early on, dancing. But I seem to remember that we were able to get in under the category of dancing some of the folk dances which we learned in Sunday School. We enjoyed them, although we were not permitted, I think, to tango!

My father was a lecturer for the Band of Hope. Now the Band of Hope was a sort of secondary Sunday School. It met on Monday evenings in our church. My father was the superintendent of it, or the one who took charge of it, and we were entertained week after week with magic lantern slides showing alcohol as the 'devil in solution'. I had no doubts at all that it was a wicked thing, was alcohol. Oh yes! it was a burning issue, but it might not have been quite so burning if my father hadn't lighted the fuse. That is to say that I was an impressionable youngster and I couldn't help being impressed by the arguments he presented, and particularly the lantern slides that he showed. I see no reason why I shouldn't confess though that I was particularly fond of a young lady at the time. We used to sit in the back row and we enjoyed the lantern slides but we were rather concerned that the light shouldn't go on too suddenly!

I can remember going to church on Sunday morning and having to walk over or walk away from men lying down on Wandsworth Common still drunk after Saturday night, so I had no difficulty in appreciating the evils of alcohol. I wonder sometimes if people today are a bit hazy about what was a very real and a very considerable problem even for somebody in a non-conformist household as I was. One of the questions that I've often put to people who disagree with me is, 'Can you think of any family in which alcohol has not at some place been a menace?' And do you know, it's astonishing still to me the number of people who are prepared to say that, although it hasn't affected them personally, they haven't to go far into the family tree to find alcohol hanging from its branches. I can say this now: even my father had his own problems. His own father had to be extracted from the pub quite often on a Saturday night and I can remember people knocking on our door and asking my father to go and do the extraction.

When the war broke out, I was eleven. I now realise that suddenly the world shut in on me and I lived as an adolescent in an enclosed world. That is to say, the information as to what was going on in this big world was almost limited to the shrapnel that dropped in our own garden. It was a closed world in another sense: we didn't know what was going on and nobody seemed to want to tell us. It was only later on when I went to Cambridge that I realised how big the world was and how different it was from the kind of world in which I had been brought up. It was the first shock of seeing the problems of becoming a Christian intellectually: I had never been confronted with any of the arguments against Christianity.

After Cambridge I suppose I sailed into the Old Kent Road just sort of assuming that they would fall down in acclamation of my presence. They didn't. It did me good, but I didn't like it at the time. I found I

Donald, left, aged fourteen, with his sister Millicent and brother Meredith taken at his mother's school in Wandsworth.

didn't know much about [the poorer classes] and I found I knew even less about the environment in which they lived. I was accompanied to my first appointment by a marvellous deaconess and she took the precaution during the first week of my being there of asking me round to the slums immediately opposite the road where the church was. I'd never seen a slum. And I had only been there a few weeks when the same deaconess said, 'There's a man over the road trying to commit suicide. Will you come and help him?' I went across and there was this fellow standing with a razor in his hand, two children cowering in corners of the room, and his wife bleeding to death. I found that shocking and wonder how many of my sermons really came within a thousand miles of that.

I can still see the faces of some of the women meeting in the Old Kent Road which gave me first-hand evidence that they'd been knocked about. Children were knocked about. They had no access to the kind of publicity which is available today but over and over again the housewife was compelled by a half-drunk husband to have sexual intercourse and to produce yet another child. If ever there was an argument for legalised abortion, I found that in the Old Kent Road.

I found it very easy to believe, as temperance advocates said, that 'gin was the quickest way out of Manchester'; so do I believe that the escape from the Old Kent Road, temporary escape, was in liquor over and over and over again. People put up with the conditions because they could get, not roaring drunk, but sufficiently inebriated to slip over into another world at least for a little while. I would say that it is certainly a reasonable claim that the Band of Hope saved a very great many people from the evils of contemporary drinking which at that time was even worse than it is now.

It would be very dangerous to underrate the influence of the temperance movement at that time and the only criticism I would make of it, after all these years, is that had the temperance movement been more closely linked with Socialist principles, I think its effect would have been far more permanent. The many effects of drink made the people tolerate a situation in which they should have been revolutionaries.

Donald Soper went on to become a famous preacher and leading pacifist. Today he speaks regularly in the House of Lords as well as at outdoor meetings. 'If you were there, I was speaking on Tower Hill today. You see, it's no good talking about God being a loving heavenly father when most people on this planet who are His children don't get enough to eat.'

•

DORIS MOSELEY *was born in 1902, the youngest in a family of thirteen. She was brought up in Middlesbrough, Leeds and finally Sheffield. Her father, a scrap dealer, was a fierce temperance advocate.*

He was brought up very strictly, my father was, and he never drank. So many men came off the boats into the docks at Middlesbrough drunk, and whatnot, lying on the floor. He thought: 'if the children grew up like this, what a world it would be'. So he decided he would start a little circle in our front room, all the kids that I played with, me brothers and sisters as well.

He bought this magic lantern and started showing these pictures, which in those days was something marvellous to kids. Then he got this film about drink, and that started it. One day he said, 'We'll have to call this meeting something,' so it became the Band of Hope, and it went on, oh, until I was about ten. We used to have postman's knock, little games, and mother used to make buns and father used to make ginger beer. We used to come out and sing the closing hymn, 'My Drink is Water, Bright from the Crystal Sea'. Then we'd say goodnight, go home, and be a good girl or boy until next week.

Once there was about twenty children and we went down to London. My father took them to see Buckingham Palace, which was a marvellous thing in those days, and showed them the changing of the guard. We sang in that square, outside Buckingham Palace, the square with the fountain in, and we sang 'My Drink is Water, Bright from the Crystal Sea'. Quite a crowd came round to hear it and father, who always did a lot of public speaking, gave a little lecture. Then he took us round where they were drinking methylated spirits, in – I don't know what part it would be, perhaps Soho. They were laid on the pavement drinking spirits of all descriptions, and he told all us kids what effect any kind of alcohol has, you see. Then it was time to come home because it was horses and carts, you know, with seat coverings on of course. It took us, oh, all night to get home, but we were quite happy.

I think there was more drink amongst the poorer people; the richer people, they drank it in their own home, 'behind bars', I call it. When I started work at thirteen, the girls from the shop, they used to go to a pub called the Queens; 'Come with us, come on, we'll go and have a drink.' You see Saturday night, the pubs kept open all hours and we didn't close until eleven on a Saturday and they'd come straight from the shop and go in this pub and have a drink. And they'd call me all sorts of names, 'cos I wouldn't go. I daren't have gone. I'd have got murdered when I got home if I'd had, because you could smell it, you can always smell it when somebody's had a drink.

My elder brother was the first to bring home a bottle of sherry. He started work and everybody at work was drinking this stuff, so he brought a bottle. So me dad says to me, 'Oh?' Then me brother says, 'Do you want a drink?' Me dad says, 'No, I don't drink that sort of stuff, but you can have a drink.' Dad said, 'Sit in the chair and once you open it you have to drink the whole of the bottle.' So my brother did and he wasn't very well, in fact, he was very poorly. He says, 'Whatever was it?' and me dad explained that it was alcohol, what effect it had on him; you couldn't even ride a bike, and your brain went funny. So me brother threw the bottle in the ash bin and said, 'I'm never going to have any more of that stuff.' That was the first one, and it came round with each of them as they got different jobs and bought home different bottles of the stuff. Father made them drink the whole bottle and the same thing happened with all of them. So my eldest brother never had a drink again in his life, and the others didn't, none of them.

He was a wonderful man, me father, really. You appreciated everything he said. He never swore, he never hit the boys, and we all had to speak so correctly. One of my brothers couldn't say 'public'; for some reason I think he wouldn't. So one day my father took him round all the public houses in Leeds, till he said it correctly, then brought him home.

Above: William Thomas Tilton, Doris's father, a fierce temperance advocate.
Right: Doris, aged thirteen, selling flags for soldiers during the First World War.

We used to have the Salvation Army come and he used to make all the boys empty their pockets and give it to the Salvation Army. While they were emptying their pockets, me dad used to say, 'Is that all you've got?' and they used to say 'yes.' And whilst they were saying 'yes' he used to go upstairs and empty all their drawers, you see, and find all these coppers, pennies and halfpennies and whatnot underneath the paper. Then he'd say to them, 'ALL your money, not part of your money. All your money. You don't get any spending money for a fortnight now.' He was very, very strict, but very kind.

Well, my father's magic lantern started me off reciting, you see. All my brothers played an instrument and my sisters all sang, and we had a concert party every Saturday night and me, I couldn't sing. Anyway, mother said, 'You've got to do something, you all must do something.' I says, 'I don't want to sing, I can't sing.' Mother said, 'Well, what would you like to do?' I said, 'Talk – recite.' I used to recite 'A drunkard stood in his cheerless home in deep distress it seemed/For poverty and want had come where hope and joy once gleamed.' And the kids used to clap, and I thought it was wonderful, being clapped at four years old.

Doris got married in a spiritualist church that her father help found and of which she is a lifelong member. She is now widowed. She writes poetry regularly, and her temperance principles remain very important to her. 'I've never been in a public house at all. I have been in a hotel but I wouldn't go in for a meal unless it was separate from the bar.'

KATE GARRETT *was born out of wedlock in London in 1899. Her mother was nineteen and Kate was adopted by a rich, childless couple. After two years, however, her mother married and reclaimed Kate. Her mother and step-father, who both had drinking problems, had met in a pub. He had run away from a Lincolnshire farming family to join the army. Although they were well educated, their drinking habits led them to a life of unemployment, poverty and violence.*

My very first memory was being in a great big bed all alone at night. My parents were out ... they used to go out to the pub every night and leave me. I was, I don't know, I couldn't have been more than three or four, and I woke up and it was night time and I saw on the walls, on both sides of the room, enormous flickering shadows, like things with wings flapping up and down. I didn't know that it was the fire – there was a fire in the room and the flames were leaping up and down and I didn't know what shadows were – I didn't know anything about anything. I just lay there frozen with terror thinking these great things on either side of the wall would slowly come at me. I didn't know till ages afterwards that they were shadows from the flickering flames.

My mother was Jekyll and Hyde. She was an absolute charmer when she was sober but a terror when she'd been to the pub. So I went in fear of my mother. Many a time she kept a cane on the table and the worst thing was if I'd done something she thought was wrong, really wrong, she would send me upstairs and say, 'I'll come and see you later.' And she'd keep me waiting for an hour to come up with the cane. I didn't really like my mother at all. Later in life I felt sorry for her, when I could understand more.

They were both educated people, but they both drank and gambled. It was hell, because my mother would scream and shout at my dad, and she was a convent school girl – she'd been at a convent boarding school till she was seventeen. Where she got the language from I'll never know but she used to call him dreadful names. And then all the china that was on the sideboard or on the kitchen table would be hurled, all this would go on. I used to stand in the corner and pray – 'please God make her go to sleep, please God make her go to sleep, please God make her go to sleep' – because I knew when she fell on the bed in a drunken stupor, we'd all get a bit of peace.

I felt so ashamed because in the street where I lived, which was a poor street, it was accepted that your dad came home on Saturday night from the pub at midnight and he blacked your mother's eye and then fell into bed. But not your mother – mothers were sacred, mothers were looked up to. I would go to church on Sunday morning and meet my pals and they would say, 'Your mum wasn't half drunk last night.' I can't tell you the shame. It really was quite dreadful.

I remember coming home one day when I was about seven. We didn't have a house but in those days poor people could rent rooms. We had two rooms and kitchen, and there were one or two, I suppose, quite decent bits of furniture in it. I came home from school and there was nothing left except the kitchen table and three chairs and two beds, because the broker's men had come in [for their debts]. I thought I'd gone to the wrong house.

I think my mother drank for the reason, drink brings forgetfulness. For an hour, two hours, you're on a high, you're in a different world. Everything looks rosy. You forget your aches and pains and then of course it's a drug, an addictive drug. So it was a mixture, I suppose, of social reasons and drug addiction. She was very pretty; clever and bright when she was sober. She thought she'd married beneath her. She was disappointed. She didn't forgive him.

Kate started to work at the age of thirteen, when still at school, cleaning the front steps and brasses of the large Kensington houses for twopence a day. As a child she 'used to pray that God would change me and I could run away and be a cabin boy on a ship'; and in 1917 she joined the army by becoming a WAAC. Two years later she met Hugh, a South African soldier eleven years her senior. They were married, Kate lying about her age, and eventually settled in Rhodesia.

All we could have for our wedding breakfast was egg on chips and tea. There were no drinks, nothing like that; we had it in the pub, but no drinks. And then we went and spent a week with a friend of my mother's that I'd written to. She ran a boarding house for munitions workers near Southampton. It was freezing cold and we had no money, so we sat up in bed reading to each other from the *Pickwick Papers*. We had an uproarious time taking it in turns, and that's how we spent most of our honeymoon.

I look back now and think that half his charm must have been that he lived eight thousand miles away. He had to go home first, and he went ahead of me by about a month, so I had to go out alone on this ship. I can still see my mother – she came to the ship to say goodbye – and I can still see her, she was little like me, standing there all alone, and she looked so forlorn. I felt really sorry for her – I wept over the rail for her. And it was such a strange thing because years, years, years, later, my daughter – who was a London hospital trained nurse – went to British Columbia. She had a job to go to, but she went alone on an immigrant ship. This was in the middle fifties, and I stood there on Liverpool Pier alone and watched that little figure get gradually smaller. It was total history repeating itself.

Anyway, one Saturday the All Blacks came to Bulawayo from New

Kate in 1918 in her WAAC uniform standing between her father (right) and Hugh whom she married the following year.

Zealand, and rugby is *the* game in Rhodesia. There wasn't any soccer, only rugby. My husband said he was going to the rugger match and that he would be home a bit late, you know, for supper, which was normally between six and seven. I got it all ready and I waited and I waited until about half past twelve, midnight. I thought I heard something outside and I went and opened the front door and he was crawling on his hands and knees up the front path, speechless. That was the first time.

He also used to get aggressive and suicidal. We had two rifles and two revolvers in the house, heaven knows why. I think men, Rhodesian and South African men, always had to have guns. When he was half drunk you never knew what he was going to do and he was always saying he was going to shoot himself. My next-door-neighbour, who was a bit light-hearted, said, 'Oh, I should let him get on with it.' And I said, 'Yes, but then I've got this horrid feeling the he might decide he wants Dominy and me to go first.' I was a little afraid, especially at night. I used to lie on the edge of the bed, waiting to fly, to pick up Dominy and run out of the house.

I told my sister-in-law about all the dreadful things that were happening. I said, 'He's taken to drink!' which was horror to me after my childhood. And she said, 'He hasn't taken to it, Tommy' – they called me Tommy because that was my army name – 'He hasn't taken to it, Tommy, he's gone back to it.' Apparently when they lived in Durban he used to go off on benders for three days at a time, but while he was in the army and while he was in England, he didn't. I think being with this crowd of men and with nothing else to do in the bush of an evening when work was over … It was horrifying, frightening.

He wouldn't give it up once he started again, and one day I started having a go myself and my tipple was Cape brandy. Now the Cape brandy that we had was the pure grape; it was cheaper than trying to adulterate it because the grapes grow almost wild at the Cape. But what we got was not beautiful matured brandy in the cask, it was fire-water – it was new. The South Africans call it 'dop', and I started drinking 'dop' and found I could keep up with him. But one morning my daughter, who was two years old, walked in the door – came in and did something a little bit silly and I slapped her for the first time. And I thought, 'Right, this is it, this is history repeating itself. Dominy is going to grow up with a drunken mother and a drunken father. We can't do it.'

It was pretty depressing really because I realised then how easy the slippery slope was. I kept wondering, how long will it be before I get like my mother? Because when I slapped Dominy – she didn't cry – she just stood there with great big round astonished eyes, as if she was trying to work out what was this thing and why had it happened. So, that's why I came away.

Taking her daughter with her, and tricking her husband into staying behind, Kate
fled to England. But it was the middle of the Depression and jobs were scarce. She
got into the habit of writing down her thoughts and observations, and after a series
of casual cleaning and clerical jobs she was encouraged by a friend to send an
article to the Daily Mirror.

I was so surprised by return of post to get a letter from the Features
Editor saying he agreed with every word I had written and would I go
and see him. I did, and he asked me about myself and then said, 'We're
going to print this and we'll give you seventeen guineas.' I nearly fainted.
I'd never seen so much money all at once. And they didn't alter a comma.
   Then the mail started coming in, sacks of it, all kinds of people
telling me their troubles. And so, in the end, I went as Agony Aunt. Kate
Garrett became 'Mary Brown'. Once I saw a billboard outside a stationer's
shop. It said: 'Read Mary Brown today. The wisest woman in England.'
It terrified me, it really did. An American journalist, who came over to
do a piece about the English press, took me to lunch and referred to me
in his article as the '*Daily Mirror*'s Sob Sister – the best in the business'.
So we were 'sob sisters' in those days, 'cos that was an Americanism.

'*Mary Brown – Sob Sister*'.

There were so many letters relating
to drink, from the man who drinks all
the money away, the man who comes
home and batters his wife, or the woman
too who goes off and leaves the kids
alone at night while she's out in the pubs.
But the people that did the drinking
didn't write to me, it was the people that
had to put up with it all who wrote to
me. All I could do was try to tell them
that I'd suffered the same thing myself,
and that in time they would learn to
cope with it, and if they really wanted
to, they would find a way.

Kate Garrett remarried in 1948 to a man she met through her agony column. 'Oh
lucky me, the kindest man in the world – he really was.' She is now a widow,
living in a small retirement home, and her sight is failing. But she knows that her
success drew on a lifelong experience of struggle. As she told Lord King, the
Mirror*'s then chairman: 'Mr King, I've done everything the readers have done.*
I've had a failed marriage; I've had to fight for, literally fight for a tuppenny loaf
of bread; I've been hungry and I've been a drunk; I've been disappointed and I've
been out of work with a daughter, no child benefits at all in those days. So I can
sit down and put myself in the reader's place.'

ALF RAZELL *also found alcohol could give temporary escape. But for him the escape was from the horrors and tedium of the trenches when he was fighting in the First World War. Born in 1897, Alf had two brothers. His father died when he was young and his mother worked as a cook. When the First World War started, he joined up as a volunteer, mis-stating his age.*

The first time was when I went in the beer canteen and they put a pint down and I struggled to drink it. But by the time we'd been there a month or so we'd be having our pint every night and we began to like it.

You occasionally had people who were staunch teetotallers, but most of them drank. Most of them would be like myself, they just joined in with others. And of course when we got to France it was the only amusement or pastime, if you like, because there was nothing else to do. We were always waiting for a Blighty, as we called it, a wound that wasn't too bad but sent you home to England. We just drank anything that came along, whisky or rum. It was illegal to supply the troops with spirits but the French, they served it on the quiet. Not in the pubs, of course, not in the *estaminets*, but in private houses. You soon knew where you could get a drink of cognac; they used to serve it in egg-cups. An egg-cup-full for six sous.

Alf, aged two, sitting on his recently widowed mother's knee.

The infantry used to hate the military police because the military police didn't go in the trenches; they were always behind the line. In fact we heard that they got leave about every three months and some of ours didn't get leave in two years. We looked upon them as wanting to stop us enjoying ourselves when we got out of the line. And I remember one night in the *estaminets*, we were enjoying ourselves, and the sergeant came in – mounted policemen, their horses were outside – he came in and they were looking for forbidden spirits. He picked up this fellow's glass of beer and smelt it. Of course the chap it belonged to was very annoyed. He picked his beer up and said, 'Keep your nose out of my beer,' and flung it over the sergeant. So the sergeant said, 'You're under arrest.' Well of course he couldn't be arrested with all the crowd of infantrymen there.

He yelled for his colleagues, they came in, somebody ran outside and drove the horses off, so it was a proper mêlée, you know, free for all.

The next day we had to have an identification parade, the whole regiment. The military policeman walked up and down the lines; he looked the worse for wear. But he didn't recognise anybody, so he told the colonel 'No'. The colonel said, 'I didn't think it would be my battalion.' But as soon as he had gone the colonel said, 'I didn't think it would be my lads, but you are all fined a hundred francs, stopped out of your pay, to pay for the damage!'

In the winter we used to get a rum station – in the summer we got lime juice – and the NCO was given the rum ration for his section. I used to dish it out to my section in a tablespoon. But those two tablespoons in the winter when you were frozen, probably wet through up to here in water or mud, well, it was life-saving, I think. Because it made them quite canned, those couple of tablespoons, under those circumstances. They began to be whistling and talking and even singing sometimes.

When you had your rum ration it certainly got you going again; it was a pick-me-up. You began to feel your feet and fingers were there. Because I remember if you undid your buttons or anything else, in the winter there, you couldn't do them up, your hands were that numbed. You had to stay out there all the time. We just dried or got wet according to the weather. We were like animals in the field.

There was only supposed to be enough rum for each man's ration, but of course with casualties, it went up and down. Sometimes in your section you only had half a dozen men, so the practice was, it was forbidden of course, you put the surplus in one of the water bottles. Well, I fell in the cart once, because I had to go back with the water-gathering party as we were short of water. I shook one water bottle and it was full, so I thought, 'I'll take that with me'. When we were halfway along the communication trench, I thought, 'I'll have a drop of that water now,' and I took a huge swig. It was rum, pure rum. Nearly choked me. Somebody, I don't know who it was, had put rum in their water bottle. Anyway I carried on, liking it and feeling OK, and I had another swig. When I got back with the party, I flopped into a shelter and went to sleep.

I remember one of the chaps waking me up: 'I should wake up if I were you, Corp, there's shelling.' I said to him, 'What's the time?' He said, 'Time? This is Tuesday, you've been there twenty-four hours.' Just then our young lieutenant came along and he said, 'Hello Corporal! Oh, you are in the land of the living again – what happened?' I told him. 'You idiot,' he said, 'do you know you could have been shot at dawn.' For being in the trenches drunk, I could have been shot at dawn. I said, 'I know.' Anyway, I never swigged rum after that.

Alf married Winifred in January 1919 while he was home on leave.

Well, we looked forward to the rum because it ironed out some of your worries, just temporarily, because we didn't have enough to make us really intoxicated. It just made you a wee bit elevated, you know? In the *estaminets*, well, we all thought that we were only on this earth a short time, in the infantry anyway, and it was one way of spending your time and forgetting a bit. If you could walk home to your barn feeling in a jolly mood, you slept all night no matter about the discomforts or anything.

Drink was the thing that men dreamed of: 'When we get out, we will have a good old drink.' 'When we go so and so, we will have a nice drink.' 'We'll have a party after the war and we will have all the drink we want.' Things like that. It was in their dreams.

After the war Alf Razell had a successful career as an engineer. Since his retirement he has lived in Watford with his wife. They both enjoy a drink before lunch.

4 Surf and Turf

The pub may have been the most readily available place of entertainment outside the home in the first decades of this century, but there were also plenty of other opportunities for ordinary people to enjoy themselves. We focus on just two of them here.

Of outdoor activities, walking the hills, fishing the rivers and canals, and cycling the then almost equally quiet country roads were all popular. Gardening, and often sewing and dressmaking too, brought pleasure as well as fulfilling family needs. Sport was more a male world. Football was played by men and boys everywhere, the street included, and was already the leading spectator sport, with betting on the pools spreading rapidly. Cricket took its place in summer; but tennis provided a rare mixed sport for women as well as men. Summer too was the time for group excursions, organised by the local Sunday Schools, pubs and factories: typically a trip to the seaside – or a day at the races.

The seaside brought together outdoor and indoor fun. One of the biggest changes in the first half of the century was the building of cinemas throughout the country, which provided entertainment for women and children as well as for men: by the 1930s, twenty million cinema tickets were being sold each week. Dancing was also one of the most popular pleasures and many towns saw new ballrooms opened during the same years. But the best place of all to dance was by the sea.

At the turn of the century paid holidays were exceptional, but after 1938 over eleven million workers were legally entitled to at least a week's annual paid leave. This was the basis of the rise of the tourist industry, the group package and the holiday camp. But for the moment the destination remained close by. With factory industry concentrated in the north, the most popular resort of all was Blackpool. It was well established as a holiday town by the 1890s, when the Victoria Pier, the Tower and the Great Wheel were built. From 1925 the famous Blackpool illuminations became a permanent feature, after a temporary halt during the Great War, and extended the summer season well into the autumn. The pleasures of sea and fresh air combined with all the fun, including the ballrooms, drew crowds in their millions. By the late 1930s the town had over seven million visitors a year and on August Bank Holiday 1937, half a million trippers arrived in 50 000 motors and 700 trains, 425 of them 'specials'.

Most people who went to the seaside for overnight or weekly holidays stayed in boarding houses or bed and breakfast establishments. The seaside landlady became an almost mythical figure, ruling her domain with a firm hand and all-seeing eye.

SARAH HAMMEL who was born in October 1897 in Padiham, Lancashire, had long wanted to be a landlady and her wish came true when in 1941 she left her home town to run a guest house in Blackpool. She was one of seven children, with four sisters and two brothers, and her father was a loom supervisor in the textile mills, where her mother had also worked before marrying. Sarah began working in the mill at the age of eleven, going to school part-time until she was thirteen, then left to work in the mill full-time. It was at this age that she went on her first trip to Blackpool.

We came from the mill where I worked, thirty of us, on the half-day excursion, as you called them in those days. On the train, for two shillings. I thought it was lovely, especially the sea, because the tide was in at the time. There were no sea wall or anything like that then and there weren't a promenade like there is now. There were rock stalls and sweet stalls with little bits of junk, but we just bought some rock. Then after that, six of us got into a landau and had a ride along the promenade, there and

back, for a shilling each, which was very enjoyable. And then after that we wandered round Blackpool and then we had to go back on the train at six o'clock.

There was always plenty going on and plenty of fun, and that's why they came, especially the Lancashire people from the mill towns. That was all they could afford, come to Blackpool. It was really a holiday and a relaxing holiday for them, although they only got a week's holiday. And they didn't get holidays with pay in those days. They had to pay for their own holidays. They had to save up every week, and deny themselves other things to get the money together for a holiday. They were only poorly paid were the textile workers in those days. We used to save two and six a week to come to Blackpool. Of course, it is a lot dearer today than what they used to be, but their wages are higher for one thing now. It used to be a happy holiday place for working people. All the Lancashire people used to come to Blackpool for what they called 'Wakes Week'. The children with their buckets and spades. It was a family holiday place.

Well, my ambition was to come here some day to live. And for a lark we had our fortunes told. She told me I'd come to live at the seaside and I would live until I was ninety, and I'd get married to the boy that I'd come to see in Blackpool. And her words came true. So I worked and I worked and I worked and saved, after we was married, till we came to Blackpool and I got my wish.

I came to Blackpool in 1941 and it was twenty-five soldiers in my guest house, so that was my war work – looking after the soldiers. And I treated those boys as if they were my own sons.

Well, after the war finished, then we started on 'apartments'. 'Apartments' was bring your own food and charge so much a night. It was two shillings a night for sleeping and then they brought their own food for you to cook. Sometimes it was like a harvest festival – some'd bring cabbage, some bring cauliflower, potatoes and meat, and then you'd cook that for them. But soon I said to them, 'Now, I'll make the dinners for you and charge you so much for your dinners.' And I did.

Everything was rationed up to 1947. They didn't finish the rationing when the war finished. Up to 1947, we was rationed with food. We were allowed so much tea and sugar from the Food Ministry, and of course I was using more tea than what I should have done. So the food inspector came to see us. He says, 'Do you know how much tea you have to make out of a pound of tea?' I said, 'Yes, one hundred and fifty cups of tea out of a pound of tea.' I said, 'Can you do it?' And he didn't answer me, so I got away with it. I also charged sixpence for the cruet on the tables; well, they used to take 'em – you'd be surprised what they used to take from the table. Salt pot or pepper pot, or spoons and forks.

Top: Sarah, first left, aged fifteen with friends in the textile mill at Padiham, near Burnley, where she worked as a shuttler. Above: Sarah at the age of thirty, seven years after she married.

I used to have a double room just for girls, you know – and double rooms for the boys – but not to sleep together. But I found out they were going to one another's bedrooms, you see, so they had a cross on their names afterwards, and I didn't take them again.

It was after the war and there was a young man and he knocked – late at night – ont' door and asked if I had any room. I says, 'How long do you want it for?' 'Oh,' he says, 'just for the night. I'm on leave.' But he wasn't in soldier's clothes, he was in civvies. So I said to my husband, 'There's a young man at the door wants a night's accommodation – what about it?' 'Oh,' he says, 'please yourself what you do.' So I took him in. And he had a little parcel with him. So I took him to the bedroom and he says, 'Do you want paying now for bed and breakfast?' And I says, 'No, it'll do in the morning when you leave.' And a few minutes after, out he went.

Our living room was facing the front door – I always kept that door, our middle door, open so as I could see people come in and out. So in came this young man with a young girl. Well, I thought she was young anyhow – about twenty or something – and they went upstairs. I heard this here rattling on the bedroom floor, so I said to my husband, 'Eh,' I says, 'I think they're getting into bed.' He says, 'Well, you've taken him in – take him out.' 'No,' I said, 'you go upstairs.' But he wouldn't, so I went and knocked on the door. He wouldn't open the door. So I went down to my husband and I said, 'You'd better go upstairs and get those two out.' I said, 'They have the door locked.' So he went knocking on the door. They wouldn't open the door, so he said, 'Well, if you don't open I shall bring the police.' So with that they opened the door, and of course they had been in bed. So this man said to my husband, 'Is this what you get for fighting for you?' And my husband says to him, 'I bet you've never ever seen a gun! I was in the 1914 War, four years and a half.' He said, 'And I knew how to behave myself.' So out they went. When they'd gone, I picks this parcel up off the dressing table, and we opened it. It was an empty box. And that was supposed to be a present for his friend!

We used to wait up in turn and lock the front door when all the guests were in. We said, 'It's your turn tonight to sit up' – because you had to be up early in the morning to get the day going really – get the breakfast made and served and do all the washing up. I had no help at all.

Well, it was like home to a lot of them. They did what they liked and as long as they was clean and reasonable and came in, you know – time they should have – then it was all right. But anybody that went over the lines, came in drunk, I wouldn't have them in again. If they wrote for accommodation the year afterwards, I used to say I was full up even if I wasn't. I wouldn't have them.

And they'd come because it was homely. They could please themselves and we used to entertain them at night. My daughter played the piano, and I sang for them, and if anybody could do a recitation or anything like that they used to get up and do it. I never had to advertise and I was always full up. I'd every bedroom full every year. And when they were going they'd say – 'Book us in for next year.'

Sarah continued running her guest house until 1949, when she retired. Her husband worked as a groundsman in a private club until he was eighty-three years old. He died in 1984. Their daughter, and only child, has now also died. Sarah still lives in Blackpool, now in sheltered accommodation. Her eyesight has faded, but her singing voice is just as clear and strong as it was when she entertained her guests fifty years ago.

TOM REDFERN *was born in September 1899 in Derbyshire, the youngest of five children – four boys and one girl. His father was a vet and his mother a teacher before she married. All his family were musical and as a young singer himself Tom took the great Caruso as his model. He went to Manchester Grammar School, leaving at the age of fifteen, and ran away from home a few years later to fight in the First World War. In 1919 he returned, relatively unscathed, and in that same year began his love affair with Blackpool.*

I came home demobbed – you got a month's demobilisation pay, and me mother said to me, 'I'll take you away.' And she took me to Blackpool, for a week. I went to the circus and she took me all along the promenade and on the old trams. And then I went into the Tower and saw the animals and the dance floor, and that got me used to liking Blackpool.

When I came out of the army, they gave you an army suit or two pounds ten shillings. So I come home and my dad, when he saw it on, he said, 'Where d'you get that suit from?' I says, 'The army's given it to me.' He said to me, 'Do you know any good tailors?' And he gave me two white five-pound notes and he says, 'Get down to Manchester.' And I went to Boydell's and I was rigged out for ten quid with a suit, an overcoat and shoes – for ten pounds. I'd a lovely grey suit, it was a stripey grey, and didn't I look a dandy after that?

My mother, she used to inspect us when we used to go out on a Sunday or anywhere special. She used to see that we had lovely good clothes, which were bought for us you know. We always went out with kid gloves – chamois gloves. She bought us ebony cane sticks and we used to wear spats. So we were smart. In the summer I used to wear my straw hat and my blazer and cream flannels. I used to have a cord at the back of my straw hat so if it blew off like a lid, well, you only had to grab it on again – it didn't fall on the floor, did it? And I'll tell you another thing I used to do – you used to have a metal container you could buy for sixpence, put water in it and keep a flower in it, so it would last all day in your buttonhole.

Tom, right, relaxing on the beach at Blackpool in 1924 with, from right to left, Annie, his mother, his future wife Lilian and Mary, her mother.

A girl wouldn't go out with you if you was poorly dressed – would they hell! They were very particular, girls in my day. I was never short of girls when I was a young man – they used to fall for me. I used to say to them, 'Good evening – are you coming in the ballroom?' Or I'd say, 'Would you like an ice cream?' So we used to go to Pavlow's, where they give you a damn big ice cream for a tanner. So, I'm afraid I was a bit of a flasher. Girls in those days, they could never be better. They were straight. They liked a bit of fun but they had good morals above all things, and they expected good morals off you. Ninety-nine per cent were like that, no no, no fiddling about. They were lovely girls.

Then I was advised by my doctor – I'd got this trouble with my feet – to learn dancing. So I went to Finnegan's in Manchester and I learnt to dance. I had a dancing partner, and I asked her her name and she said Rose. And she said, 'What's your's?' And I said, 'My name's Arthur Davenport' – but I told her the wrong name. Well, in those days they always used to want to grab fellows. You see their boyfriends had been to the war and a lot of them didn't come back. They'd lost their sweethearts and they'd been without boys for four years. So they were looking for husbands. We used to say, 'Don't tell them your name. Tell 'em another name.' So I knew a fellow in the army named Arthur Davenport, he'd come from Stockport, so I told her his name.

Anyhow, I said to her, 'Would you like to come to Blackpool?' She says, 'Why?' I says, 'They're running trains there.' I said, 'I should tell your old man you'll be late.' It was half a crown to go on the train and half a crown to go in the ballroom – so for five shillings you'd a wonderful night, didn't you?

Tom in the Royal Engineers, 1917. He was a wireless telegraphist.

I used to go there in my blazer and my lovely cream white shirt and beautiful clean white tie. Lovely clothes I had, lovely flannels. And dance all night long while eleven. I had to put me shoes in my pocket 'cos I used to wear canvas white shoes with my white suit. But you can't dance in those, so I used to put me brown shoes on to dance because I could slip on the floor. And I've danced all night there, aye.

So we used to dance there while eleven o'clock, then get the half past eleven train back to Victoria Manchester, and then I'd take this girl all the way home and then walk home meself. I wouldn't get home while two in the morning. Oh God, my old man used to play hell. He had to come down in his night-shirt to open the door. He let me brothers have a key, but he says, 'You're too wild, you are.' I was rather wild, I'm afraid. My mother said, 'Why can't he have a key, our Tom?' Mother was a bit soft with me, by the way. He said, 'Well, he's too wild. Coming home at two in the morning. Where the hell does he get to?'

Anyway I brought this Rose home and my dad says to me, 'Where did you get that girl from?' She was very smartly dressed, beautiful red clothes on, red gloves, red stockings, red shoes – ooh blimey – I thought, who's this coming up? Anyway, my father says to me, he says, 'Eh,' he said, 'why don't you go and find a proper lady?' I said, 'What's wrong with her?' 'Oh,' he said, 'some day you'll settle down like the others.' So I said, 'Oh, I don't want to settle down yet.' Anyway, he says to me, 'Go and see Jim Elm's daughter.' So I said, 'Jim?' He said, 'Well, she's grew up with you as a little girl, Tom. You both went to the same Sunday School, both went to the same day school. Go and take her out instead of going … into town Sunday night "monkey parading".' He said, 'Go on – take her t'pictures.' So I go up to this house where she lived, and she looked at me. I said, 'Good evening.' She said, 'Come in, Tom.' Well, I sat talking to her and then I plucked up the courage. I said to her, 'Would you like to go to the pictures with me?' 'Oh,' she said, 'I'd be delighted.' And that's how I started with my wife. And I never saw that girl – the dance girl – again. Never.

When we were courting my mother said to me, 'Mrs Elm wants us to go to Blackpool, Tom. Will you come with us?' She said, 'Lilian's going too.' So we go to Blackpool and my mother'd have a room and then Lilian had one and I'd have another room. And we used to all go out together. Or my mother and her mother used to go shopping and Lilian and myself used to go on the promenade. And sometimes we'd say, 'We'll have a meal out, mum. We won't come in to dinner, come home tonight.' And then we'd go and have a bit of a cuddle – in one of the sand dunes. There was boys and girls, many'd go up there, and there were little coves where the waves used to come in – and you'd sit there and have a cuddle an' all. Not bad.

It was ten and sixpence a day, full board. Hey, ten and sixpence! Full board! In those difficult times. I'll tell you, from the day I was married we had a week's holiday every year, and you didn't get your holiday pay then by the way. You saved up for it – that's how you were in those days. Your mother and grandmother and grandfather saved up for a week's holiday, and that's why they enjoyed it. They'd scraped and saved their coppers for the holiday, and they enjoyed it.

When we were married we went to live with Lilian's mother and grandmother, so I had my mother-in-law with me from 1927 to 1956. Never went anywhere without her, and she was a wonderful woman. We went to Blackpool nearly every year. She had relatives at Rhyl, you know, but we used to like Blackpool. We used to always stay in Alexander Road. They knew us, and we knew them. We used to love it. And sometimes Lilian's mother would stop in – she'd say, 'I'm not going out tonight Lilian, I'll stop in.' So I'd say to my wife, 'Come on kid – let's go to t'Ballroom.' And we'd have an evening there while the old lady would be with the guests in the guest house.

I'll tell you why I liked Blackpool. First of all the boarding house people, they welcomed you. When you go to Blackpool, you'll see Tom, Dick and Harry, the general people, all smiling and enjoying themselves. At holiday. And the air is like wine. You can drink it in, you can feel it when you go to Blackpool. Get on the promenade and inhale the ozone and it's like wine. You're a new person, you really are. The sea in those days was nice to swim in – I mean you couldn't swim in it now, could you? When I went with Lilian I'd get up in the morning and I'd go for a walk on the prom and I'd have five oysters for a shilling before me breakfast. Five! Put them down. Me wife, she's looking at me – 'I don't know how you could eat them.' 'Oh, they do you good, these.' Five for a shilling! Can you imagine!

You've got everything you want at Blackpool, haven't you? You can have a night-club, you can have dancing, you've got the fairground. There's nothing that you can't have. It's your own fault if you don't enjoy yourself at Blackpool.

Tom and Lilian did not have any children and after thirty-two years of marriage she died unexpectedly in 1959. He was devastated by her death and had to give up his work at Avros, the aircraft manufacturer. He moved to Wales and eventually took up part-time work in the Prestatyn Bus Depot, where he stayed until his early seventies. He continues to live in Prestatyn on his own, leading an active social life with his many friends. After not wanting to go near the place which held such happy memories for him, Tom has recently returned to Blackpool, sometimes staying at the holiday camp there. But he says it is not the same. He has never remarried, proclaiming that Lilian was the only girl for him.

FRED ROY *was born in October 1901 in Newcastle upon Tyne, where his father was a painter and decorator. When he was six years old, his parents took over a small hotel in Blackpool which belonged to a relation who had died. Fred had two older brothers and the whole family helped run the hotel. It was in the kitchens that Fred learnt a new skill and became interested in the possibilities of show business.*

Blackpool's a big show town, so of course anybody would be fascinated with show business. It soon brings you out if you live in Blackpool. When I got about ten years of age, I used to peel the potatoes for the hotel. In the summer time we'd have about thirty people in, and my job was to peel the potatoes for the guests. I used to start the night before and this got very, very boring, continually peeling potatoes, so I used to keep throwing them up and catching them and throwing the knife up and trying to catch that in the potato. And this went on for quite a long time, till eventually I could juggle three potatoes. Also, we had in the dining room a waste-paper basket. Well, I used to balance that on me foot and try to throw it up and catch it on me head. All that, and this fascination for juggling took me over.

There was the Palace Varieties, the Hippodrome Varieties and the Tower Circus at Blackpool. And I used to go and watch these jugglers work. I used to get so fascinated I used to come out before the finish and get home and try and practise some of the tricks. I remember I bought juggling clubs and some tennis balls, or some tennis racquets, and really went at it and practised and practised. I worked a few charity shows and eventually I took part in a talent competition at the Royal Pavilion Blackpool and I won first prize. So that's what started me off.

I used to go to the gymnasium in Blackpool three times a week where me brother, he was a gymnast, was practising. I met there Arthur Macilvoy, who was also keen on the stage, but he was more of a rough and tumble comic. The three of us got together and we said we'd form an act. We decided we'd call ourselves Roy Brothers and Mack. We got the *Stage* and we looked up to see if we could get an engagement, and we got offered to go to the Queen's Theatre, Farmworth, near Bolton. They offered us fifteen per cent of the company share. We got no idea what fifteen per cent of the company share was, but we thought, 'Well, we should do very well really.'

We got digs right opposite the theatre and three of us had to sleep in one bed. We used to toss up who was going to sleep in the centre. On the Monday night there was about thirty people in. So we thought, that's a start anyway. Then we discovered they were all bill-pasters. None of them had paid. So at the end of the week all we got was seventeen and six for the three of us. We had a job to pay our digs, but fortunately my brother had some money, and he'd paid the landlady. And off we went.

We did work a few more dates together, but then I went on me own and I went around all the dumps. Nearly always on shares. I never seemed to get any money, only just enough to pay me way. In some weeks I couldn't even pay the digs. I used to have to go to the landlady and say, 'Sorry, I haven't taken enough, I can't pay.' I used to pay her as much as I could and promise to send it on. Which I never did because the next week were just as bad. This went on for months like that.

Nearly all the double acts were man and wife teams. The first time I saw my wife was before I came in the business. I remember going to the Tower Circus, Blackpool, and seeing some trick cyclists called the Bale family, and seeing this girl going into a big loop which was strapped to her father's back: he cycled around the stage and she looped the loop inside. Now many years later when I was with the Ashley Stage Circus, the Bale family including her joined the circus at Bootle. Eventually we got very friendly together, and I remember we were walking home one night with Mr Bale and I asked if I could marry his daughter. He didn't seem so keen on it, you see, because they don't like splitting the act. That was the trouble. But eventually he said OK.

Fred, back row, second left, at an end of tour party at the Theatre Royal, Stockport, in 1922. The show was E. G. Bale's Royal Continental Stage Circus and Fred's future wife Daisy is sitting in front of him.

We was playing at Darwen in Lancashire at the Theatre Royal with the Royal Continental Stage Circus at the time. We got married at Kirkham and then we went on to Blackpool for the reception. After the wedding we went back to Darwen and worked that night with the circus. It was those days.

She was a very good performer, very good performer indeed, good personality, and we soon fitted together. If you marry in the business like that, it's easy. Unfortunately she wasn't educated, had never been to school, and so she was a bit backward, like most of these circus people were. You see, they were more concerned about how many balls you could juggle, or how many somersaults you could do, than learn to read

Fred performing his juggling act with his wife Daisy at the Hippodrome, Preston, in 1930. An apprentice called Ritchie is in the middle.

and write. And they thought if you got educated you'd be leaving the troupe and split them up.

The very name 'variety' means each act's different. When we were on the big time we travelled with our own backcloth, which was the interior of a sports shop. And there was a counter on the stage with various things on it. Now it looked like a real shop, and the music would be very, very soft. As the curtain went up, my wife used to be behind the counter polishing a tennis racquet. Then she'd come out front and juggle a tennis racquet and a couple of balls. Then she'd catch the tennis racquet and throw it right across the stage. And just as the tennis racquet was getting near the door I used to enter and catch the tennis racquet. Now I was dressed as a comedy sailor. I had a real parrot on me shoulder. I was carrying a fox terrier dog under me arm and a kitbag under the other arm. I just had room to catch the tennis racquet with the same arm as I had the kitbag. And of course the drummer used to give a rim shot as the racquet hit me hand. That was the entrance, a very funny entrance. Then I used to drop the kitbag and throw the tennis racquet back to the wife, and she'd be juggling three tennis racquets like that, and that's how the act more of less consisted of. Not a lot of comedy but we included the parrot, and a dog and a cat. The reason they were in the act, they were pets, and the management wouldn't let us bring them in the theatre as pets, so we decided to put them in the act.

Used to be some real dumps. Occasionally we'd get very bad digs. Some pros that stayed at some bad digs were so dissatisfied that when they left they nailed a kipper under the table. I was told that the landlady took all the floorboards up to try to find out where this smell came from.

The landladies used to have an address book and on the Sunday before you left you were supposed to write your comments, saying you'd had a jolly good week and thanks for everything, good cooking and nice landlady! That was the recognised thing, and you signed your name. But when you got very bad digs you used to praise them an' all, but at the bottom, in very small letters, you used to put, 'Quote the raven.' That meant just the opposite of what you've put. It was the sort of secret thing in the profession, but I don't think more than twice a year you'd probably do that.

The usual thing for pros when they got on the train on a Sunday morning, they would have in their hand what we called 'The Pros' Bible'. Actually it was the *News of the World*, and they used to read this practically all the journey. When we were very hard up, we couldn't afford all the fares with perhaps ten members of a little review. We had only enough money for eight, but we knew where the ticket collectors would be and would avoid them. But when we got to the town and they wanted the tickets, at the barrier, I used to have all the eight tickets in me hand. And what I used to do, was when I got to the ticket collector, I'd push all the tickets into his hand. Then one person at the back would shout out. 'Can you please tell me where John Street is please?' To put him off the scent. All the other artistes would walk through, and by the time he counted his tickets he couldn't tell what was what. That was a regular thing we did. But we got at least two through that way. And of course dogs. We always carried a dog with us most of the time and we'd cover the dog over when the conductor came to collect the tickets. Arriving at a town, we'd let the dog loose and he'd run through the ticket barrier and wait for us outside the station. That was a regular thing for pros' dogs. I don't remember ever really paying for a dog.

Pros, more or less, they're a different type of people. They got no interest much in anything else. Only the profession really. No interest in politics or anything. Only interest really in the theatrical profession, that's all. Most pros are like that. I don't know of any pro ever giving up. You never made a lot of money out of it, but you kept going: always the idea that you were going to make it and get in the big time. It's the gypsy in your blood. Once he's settled into show business, he doesn't give up. Once you're in it, you never change.

Fred continued performing, mostly in holiday camps, until the age of seventy-five. His wife, Daisy, died in 1977; they had no children. He now lives alone in Hove and is an enthusiastic bowls player. Occasionally he is asked to put on shows at bowling club dinners and he does charity performances. He still practises his juggling every day.

B lackpool and the other holiday resorts around Britain's coasts provided the most popular break from everyday existence, but a day at the races came a close second, with its heady mixture of crowds, excitement and the possibility of winning a lot of money. Horse racing, 'the sport of kings', was a national pastime which attracted people of all social classes. But the gambling that went with it had become a massive underground activity: off-course betting had been made illegal in 1853, and in 1906 street betting was also outlawed. Our three contributors recall what life was like on and off the track in the days when a rich upper-class elite ruled the all-powerful Jockey Club and bookies and tipsters commonly operated outside the law.

FRANK HILL *was born in Tunbridge Wells in 1903, starting life above the butcher's shop owned by his father. He became a scholarship boy at the local grammar school and still remembers the ignominy of having to deliver joints of meat to his father's customers on the way to school. He left school at fourteen to join his father's business.*

My father always had four or five horses. Four of them were used in the business and he kept one for himself, and naturally from a very early age I grew up with a love of horses. I remember Tunbridge Wells when there were only four motor cars and probably four hundred horses, so you can see the natural sequence.

The first race Frank ever attended was the 1919 Derby and he was hooked from then on. With his winnings and £100 from the Post Office account opened for him by his mother, he bought his first horse.

This horse had a name, Cul-de-sac. And that was about what it was. It was no damn good at all! Anyway I made myself look a bit older and a man of the world, and went down to a trainer in Lewes, named Hammond. I said, 'Mr Hammond, would you train a horse for me?' He said, 'What's it called?' I said, 'Cul-de-sac.' He said, 'Oh that's no bloody good. But,' he said, 'I've got an empty box. I didn't know what to do with it anyway. I'll do the best I can.' I said, 'How much do you charge Mr Hammond?' He said, 'Three pounds ten a week.' Three pounds, ten! And it's £220 a week with the Newmarket people today. Anyway, he looked me up and down and said, 'I think in your case, we'll say ten shillings a day.' I suppose he thought the horse wouldn't last a week. Or I wouldn't last a week! Anyway, that was exactly what I earned. My father paid me three pounds ten a week, and that was ten shillings more than he paid his best men. He thought I was absolutely spoilt – he would have given me about five bob I think. I lived at home, of course, so the whole of my income went on keeping this one horse.

Anyway, needless to say, it was no good – I ran it at Folkestone. The money ran out, the horse was no good and I sold it for thirteen guineas and went back home very heartbroken, but determined that one day I'd buy a decent one.

Getting to be a gentleman jockey is to join one of the most exclusive clubs in England. I knew that I could never get in on my own because I was only a butcher's boy. So I asked Lord Abergavenny to sponsor me – he was another horse owner. He said, 'Of course, m'boy.' And in due course the forms arrived for me to fill up. Well, my heart sank when I saw one of the first questions. It asked for rank or profession. All I could say was that I was a butcher's boy, so I had to tackle the problem in another way. I had an inspiration. I just had been made a partner in the shop by my father. It was not 'Hill and Son' any more. So I hit on the idea of putting down 'company director' as my profession! I was always cheeky. So I got accepted.

Then it came time for my first race as a gentleman jockey. We were all in the changing room getting ready to run – there were true aristocrats,

Frank, right, riding Grand Canal at Eridge National Hunt in 1930.
He went on to win the race.

like Lord Grosvenor, one of the Wellesleys, there. As we filed out, the steward yelled to me, 'Well, you're certainly not a gentleman and you'll bloody well never be a jockey.'

In the early days, of course, you didn't have the tests to check if a horse had been nobbled. And there were ways you could nobble a horse to win quite legally. If a horse had a wind problem, you could tube a horse. That meant cutting a hole into the windpipe and put a silver tube in. This was perfectly legal and really helped the horse to breathe. However, what sometimes happened was that the horse would be tubed on the morning of the race at the racecourse. To perform the operation, naturally enough the horse needed a painkiller or anaesthetic. So what was more sensible than give it a shot of cocaine. That made it into a different horse altogether and there would be no stopping it!

The build-up in the two months prior to Derby Day creates a special atmosphere. Anticipation increases as the first Wednesday in June draws near, and the actual day is unlike any others. The day starts at the crack of dawn and for the members, they are dressed up in top hat and coat. The crowds are terrific, so are the traffic jams. Anticipation is in the air.

The scene was electric – there were gypsies, tipsters, lucky heather, beggars everywhere from car park to enclosure. Even the regulars appear different on Derby Day. Friends and acquaintances turn up in unusual garb of top hat and morning suit. The women were something different with varying degrees of success! Celebrity spotting is the order of the day – royals are the top of the Hit Parade, followed by film stars and politicians. There were hurdy-gurdies, all the fun of the fair, even more then than now. On the left-hand side were the stands and boxes and on the right coconut shies, funfairs and roundabouts.

A lot of people used to go with horse-buses – later on it became double-deckers. People used them as a grandstand. Derby Day was a special day occasion in which to be seen attending. For the likes of me, it was just another racing day, we didn't want honour and glory. We wanted the money!

Then there were the 'welshers'. There were hundreds of them at the Derby. 'Welshers' were bookmakers who would stand and take your money right up to the Derby. And if an outsider won, they would stay on; but if the favourite won, they would disappear!

My wife, I won't say she liked horses, but she liked a day's racing when I took her, which was not very often. Because, unfortunately, if we'd had a good winner, the champagne used to flow, and if you hadn't had a good winner the champagne flowed even farther. So it wasn't exactly convivial company for a young lady who was brought up in the strict Wesleyan faith, was it? I'm ashamed to say not only me, but all the men gave the wives a pretty poor do. The clubs I belonged to – like the Masonic Club, Kent and Sussex, the County Club or the Constitutional, they were all full of married men. So my wife wasn't treated any differently from any of the rest, I suppose.

My latest horse is called Be Surprised. I told the trainer, when he asked me why it had such a silly name, that I would be very surprised if he couldn't win in a rotten race at Plumpton; even more surprised if I was still alive to see him win anything, and marvellously surprised if he won the Gold Cup at Cheltenham. Well, I've jumped the first two fences, and I await the third – the Gold Cup. You have to think lucky to be lucky in racing. I realise it's almost an impossible dream but there's no harm in dreaming it is there?

A serious accident in 1931 finished Frank's career as a jockey, although he continued hunting into his seventies. Until then he also carried on as a butcher, and the money he made from his successful business helped to service his passion for racing. In all he has owned 118 winners. Frank lives on his own near Tunbridge Wells, his wife having died in 1983, and has a daughter and son living nearby. He still goes to the races to watch how his horses fare.

RALPH HARRIS *was born in Leeds in 1902 of Russian-Jewish immigrant parents. His father was a tailor and despaired of his wayward son, who left school at thirteen and learned his bookmaking trade in the streets and billiard halls of working-class Leeds. Sharp and quick, he admits that his was a 'misspent youth'.*

We stayed away from work for three days and found ourselves on the racecourse. I'll never forget it! In those days jobs were short – but we couldn't care less. When we came back to the factory, the manager – he was a Jewish fellow but he was all there – said, 'Where have you lads been?' He'd already asked some of the lads that worked there, where we were, you see – we'd been missing for three days. So they said we'd gone to the races. So he said to me, 'You. I think you're the ringleader. Where've you been for three days?' 'I've been ill. I've had the doctor, had the 'flu, and all this.' He said, 'What were you doing at Wetherby Races then?' Anyway, he made no bones about it. He says, 'There's your hat and coats – you're finished.' So we got the sack.

But I was fifteen or sixteen, you see, and no job, so we used to go to the races, and we worked out all the odds – 2 to 1, 6 to 4, 3 to 1. And we learnt to tick-tack in the café from the menu. You know, on the menu each item was numbered: what price egg on toast? – one two three four five and then you go! We went back the following day and the girl wouldn't serve us. She said, 'You're not going practising on my menu.'

Ralph taking a book at Catterick racecourse, Yorkshire, in 1930.

On the racecourse the bookmaker has two tick-tacks sometimes, or one at least. It's like a Morse Code. The money that comes on horses changes, he reads the code from the tick-tack men, then he tells you the price. It's quite interesting and it's very tricky. You've got to be very quick-witted to work out everything mathematically – all in your head. It's mental. That's why you could finish up in the blooming barmy shop!

In the old days bookmaking was only legal on the racecourse. Anywhere else it was illegal. So we did our business on the racecourse. I travelled the length and breadth of Britain to every race taking bets – always by train, never drove. I could show you the books – full of bets – hundreds of them. All different. You'd take two or three hundred books in a race. At the end of the day of probably six races you would have taken two thousand bets of all types – fivers, tenners, twenties, fifties, hundreds – all types of bets.

I started as a runner, then became a bookie's clerk, then I was a bookmaker and I finished up with some the greatest bookmakers in the world.

And the jockeys; I remember Tommy Weston. He was a very common lad in his way, all these jockeys were very common. He got a job as a stable lad when he first started. I said to him, 'What do you actually do in the stables?' He said, 'I'm a separator.' So I said, 'What's a separator?' He said, 'I separate the shit from the straw.' That was his first job and he finished up owning his own house and riding for Lord Derby. But they were famous these lads, 'cos their ability was there.

I've had some of the finest ladies in the land. Slept with 'em as a young fellow. I was very friendly with a lady that her husband used to breed horses. One of her horses was having a service. And she says to me, 'Have you ever seen one of these services?' You know, having a service to a mare. So I said, 'No, I've never seen it.' She says, 'Well next Monday, so-and-so's coming in to go with so-and-so', she says. 'Well,' she says, 'it turns me on. Why don't you come?' Anyway, it was a right paraphernalia! There's two men at the back, they get the mare and lift the horse right on top of it, and then there's people in the way having champagne – having the time of their bloody life. So I said, 'No wonder it turns you on.' She was very naughty, she knew I was married. So I stayed with her a week. I had a lot of sex appeal. She sent an Interflora bouquet of flowers to the wife, and she put on it: 'Thanks for the loan of your husband!'

Ralph Harris still works as a bookie on the northern circuit as much as three or four times a week, with a clerk and three tick-tacks working for him. He also owns a night-club and because of the late hours he cannot go to bed early to this day.

ERNEST MARKE *was born in Sierra Leone in 1902 into a middle-class family. His mother was a member of a Nigerian royal tribe and was one of the first African women to complete her education in England. Ernest had a strong sense of justice and was always getting into fights defending the underdog. Eventually, he ran away from home and stowed away on a ship that was torpedoed in the First World War. Later on, he became a merchant seaman, like many others in the small black community in Liverpool.*

The first time I gambled on a horse, it all happened by accident. It was 1923, after I'd gone back to England, back to Liverpool. And it was the Derby Day. I'll never forget this, because I saw a man standing on a corner and another man looking left and right. I say, 'What's this man standing looking left and right?' I thought they were thieves. Someone say, 'No, the man is a bookmaker.' Well, gambling was illegal, you see.

The bookmaker had a watchman looking for the police. I saw people wandering up and slipping them some money and getting some slips back. I had five shillings with me, so I put on half a crown. I didn't know anything about horses and I said, 'What's the name of the horses?' They show me paper with the name of the horses. So I picked this one – and he won! I put half a crown on it. Beginner's luck! It won! I can even remember the price – 11 to 2. Which means I won over thirteen shillings. And I remember the jockey – Tommy Weston. And I remember the man who owns the horse – if anything happen to you, you remember the first time – Lord Derby. And after that I start backing horses.

Later on Ernest became a tipster, selling tips on the horses he thought would win:

I did this by being a magician, sleight of hand, that sort of thing. The moment I got a crowd, I starts spieling. 'I'm the luckiest man you ever did see. Why? Perhaps because I'm black. Black. I'm lucky, 'cos you people, you got the pluck. We black haven't. You can go up in an aeroplane. I'm frightened to get up there. Something might happen. You with your superior arms, you come to my country and capture my people and send them to America as slaves. But we still survived, so we're lucky. Oh yeah! The winners I have given you, I cannot count. How do I know all these things? Just luck. That's why they stop me on the street and tap me on the head. Black for luck. Because you know, I gotta animal that can't lose this race. And I will tell you ... I bet you'll leave this racecourse with a packet of money.'

I watch them and some of them don't give a damn, but some are interested – 'cos it's all based on psychology. You have to take that one first, then the rest follow. Because if you don't have the first punter, all the hard work of lecturing – lost! They don't want to be the first. They don't want to look a fool. So once the first one buy, you've got it. So while you're lecturing you're also watching their faces, their eyes. I work the tips the same as I work the charms. The same lecture. With the horses I sometimes make it a little bit different, more spectacular. I sell the slips for a shilling each. And sometimes when the day is over, I earn more than the ordinary man can earn in four weeks wages. But if my tips were bad, I used to run like hell to the other side of the racecourse!

Ernest learnt a lot from another black tipster, Prince Monolulu:

He was like my big brother. He taught me the tricks. When he went to Doncaster for the St Leger race, everybody know him, so he can get digs. It was very hard for the black people to get digs. He accepted me like a son or a little brother. He used to book digs and write to me. 'I've booked a room for you, son, come along.' So we sleep in the same bed, one big bed, so I know all about him. I know more about Monolulu than even his wife know. But the only thing he did was tell me off when he found out I was selling tips. I don't blame him. 'No messing about tipping, I'm the one who sell the tips around.' But I said, 'Who are we against you? You are the tops. So what you worried about?' 'Oh, well maybe you're right, dear boy.'

We called him Lulu. Tall fellow, dressed like an Abyssinian. He said he was an Abyssinian prince. He was a character, everybody knew him. He showed me the tricks of the trade. He was from St Thomas, British West Indies, but he told me, 'You better keep that to yourself. I told them I'm from Abyssinia because they respect people who've never been conquered. Abyssinia has never been conquered, so they respect me.' Lulu wore about five, six or seven feathers on his head, all different colours. He used to shout, 'I gotta horse, I gotta horse.' He was the first black man on the course and people used to say, 'My God!' They used to buy – 'black is luck!'

I remember one day in Doncaster, St Leger day in October. I had a big crowd and I was lucky. All the horses I picked that day won. So there I was making money left and right. There were three hooligans watching me all along. I knew they were hooligans. You see, when you are in my line of business, one look at a hooligan and you know. The hooligan is in the eyes. Because all your life for your own protection you've been watching the faces of people to guard yourself. You know the wicked ones – nine out of ten you will know a trouble-maker.

Now I saw these three at my pitch but none of them ever bought a ticket. I thought to myself, 'They're villains.' But what can I do? Once I've finished a pitch I let the crowd go, take a rest, start again and get a new crowd. But these three geezers kept tailing me. One of them said to the crowd, 'Oh yes, what he's telling you is a good tip.' But they never bought any from me. 'That's funny. Is my judgement wrong or what?' I'm thinking?

I just got rid of the crowd, the money in my pocket, when two of them stood up and one came to me. 'Give us a nicker.' That means a pound. Well, a pound was a lot of money in those days and you don't give them away. Give me a 'tosh', a half a crown, yes, but they asked for a pound, a nicker, just like that. Well, that was a goddamn liberty! 'What you mean, give me a nicker? Where do you think the money's coming from?' 'Don't you hear us tell the people you gave us winners. What do you think we do that for, sambo? Did we do it for our health?' They were real villains. Then they grabbed hold of me and tried to get hold of my pocket. And I'm fighting like mad. I wasn't gonna let them get hold of my money. Some women on the racecourse looked at us, and

Left: Ernest with his first wife Alma at Blackpool in 1930.
Below: Left, with a friend in Bellevue, Manchester, 1951.

they saved me – 'Leave him alone. What is he doing to you? Why don't you make your own living? You are nothing but rats!' And they pick up their shoes and started hitting them and shouting for the police. And they disappeared from the crowd.

And that same night – I never forget this – I was working the markets that night after the races. Once you had a chance to make money, you make it. I might not have another chance for months. So I was in the market selling tips for the next day, and I went to the pub to quench my thirst, right there in the marketplace. I was drinking and I felt like going to the toilet. The toilet was in the yard. And I'd no sooner got in the yard when three men left the pub and followed me. But they didn't come to urine, they came to attack me. Trying to get my money off me. I fought like mad and shouting at the same time. People in the bar could hear and the women send their men out – 'That poor black man is being attacked. Go and help him!' – and the three men ran away. Later on I was told that one of these three men was an ex-policeman, a crooked policeman who was kicked out of the police force. So in everything you find the good and the bad.

After thirty years of living life on the edge, Ernest settled down in the 1950s with his second wife, Elsie, a Bradford girl. He worked as a boilerman and became the father of five children. His love of the turf has never faded and he still follows the racing on television and lays bets at his local bookies. After retirement at sixty-five he took up writing, and is busy with his latest novel, which is based on the story of the ANC, the once outlawed political organisation in South Africa.

5 All Your Kisses Are Mine

R ight through this century, it has always been more difficult for a woman to achieve financial independence. Women today still earn little more than half an average man's wage, just as they did at the turn of the century. But their chances then were still more restricted. Scarcely any women worked in the higher professions or management. Before they were married they might at best have become teachers, nurses or clerks. More often they were unskilled factory hands or domestic servants.

On marriage the expectation was that the husband would support his wife with a 'family wage', and that she would give up paid work. Between the wars professional women, such as teachers or civil servants, were obliged to resign on marriage. And although it was rare for single working-class women never to work outside the home, there were many unmarried middle-class women who remained at home, often falling into the role of carers for older relatives, and remaining dependent on their fathers for their upkeep.

The First World War did not radically change women's situations, although their experience of more responsibility and freedom during those years raised their expectations. Even in 1928, when women were given the right to vote at the same age as men, it did nothing to redress their restricted horizons. Marriage remained women's expected 'career'.

One in seven of the women of this turn-of-the-century generation, however, never married. The chances were against them. The huge casualties of the First World War, plus emigration, meant that women outnumbered the men of their age; and their disadvantage was made worse because marriageable men tended to choose younger women – while a woman rarely married a man younger than herself.

For those many women of that generation who remained single, what was life like? The stories of our three contributors begin against the backdrop of Edwardian England. Mary Butler and Joyce Wilkins tell of a childhood very much dominated by their parents, in particular their fathers, which sowed the seeds of future unhappiness. Both of them wanted to marry and have children, but differing circumstances and events destined them to remain single. Dorothy Galton, by contrast, flew in the face of convention: she refused to compromise or conform to society's restrictions. In remaining single, she made a deliberate choice to lead her life as an independent woman.

MARY BUTLER *was born in Kilburn, North London, in June 1898. Her father was a drapers' buyer.*

My mother and father were engaged to be married for four years before they ever did marry. And my father always boasted that his home, to which he brought her, was ready down to the last tin-tack. And they were – ideally happy. There is a letter my mother wrote to her friend, that her happiness was almost too great to be borne: her dear, dear husband, her beautiful home and – I find this difficult to tell you almost without emotion – her baby, lying under her heart.

But when I was just five weeks old my mother died. And there was my poor father, left absolutely desolate. I absolutely adored my father; he was mine, and he loved me. Intensely. As a very small child, in my cot, I can remember sitting bolt upright holding onto the sides and keeping my eyes very wide open, so that I shouldn't go to sleep before he came. Just listening, till he came in. Then I would hear his key in the front door, umbrella going into the stand, hat going onto the stand, and then racing up the stairs. And then I leapt up in the cot and was gathered into his arms.

My childhood, on account of all this, was very difficult. We eventually had thirteen different housekeepers to bring me up, more or less. I'm sorry to say that many of them drank. Now in my very mature years, I think about it quite a lot, and I realise that those women's lives must have been pretty wretched, very lonely. But they never played with me.

The very first one we had was a widow with one daughter. She was a very bad-tempered woman indeed. The slightest thing you didn't do at once, she would say, 'Come here, take down your knickers,' and she'd snatch me across her lap and beat my bottom with a cane. And do you know, telling you that, I almost feel it now. I used to bite my lip and think, 'I won't cry, I won't cry, I won't cry.' Another thing she did as a punishment was shut me up in the wardrobe on the top of the stairs, with dad's winter coats – and it reeked of mothballs. I hated being locked in there; I hated the smell of mothballs, and I hate the smell of mothballs to this very day.

Lots of people have said to me, 'Why didn't you tell your father?' But somehow or other, it was a sort of 'you must never worry daddy.' Also, when he came home, and I was there, in his arms, and being loved, I think all the horrors of the day just faded away. I am sure they did.

I was a very lonely child till I went to school; very lonely child, but full of imagination. I used to imagine all sorts of things: one of the things I did was to play church on the stairs – with the dolls. When I was five I went to the kindergarten. And then eventually I was sent to the high school, which was very much a 'select seminary for young ladies'. I was

absolutely hopeless at things like maths but get me onto English literature, and elocution, and I was top of the class always. I adored that: 'Mary Butler, please come out and show them how it ought to be done.'

My one idea of when I grew up was to be an actress. But as for father, to be an actress was just one step away from the streets! 'Be an actress? Of course you can't be an actress, you're going to business college and you're going to become a secretary' – which was an absolute disaster for me. The whole thing was homework, homework, homework. Adding up, columns of figures like this, you know? It was too utterly awful. I practically had a breakdown and then my poor father thought, 'What am I going to do with this girl?'

My first little love affair. Yes dear, I will tell you. We met when I was about seventeen. He was my cousin Ned's school friend. He was tall and dark and handsome – no nonsense about that, he really was. He used to write to me nearly every day. And all of a sudden, my father said to me, 'What are these letters you keep having?' So I said, 'They're my friend, they're Ned's friend, and he's in love with me.' So dad said, 'Let me see some of them.' Well, when I think – how innocent they were. There was nothing vulgar, nothing, well, to use today's overworked word, nothing sexy about it at all. Nothing. I look back on it and think it was sweet innocence. There's no doubt about it.

But of course my father said, 'That is all nonsense.' He said, 'What can you know about love? You don't know anything about love! You don't know what love means!' And I said, 'But I love him daddy, you see

I love him!' So he told me that I was to tear up all the letters. Put all this nonsense out of my mind. So when he came home the next night, I was able to tell him truthfully that all the letters were torn up and put into the kitchen stove. Burnt. Which of course I did.

My father was such an enormous influence on me. I've often looked back and thought, 'If my mother had been here the whole thing would have been treated so differently.' I can imagine her saying, 'Oh don't be so silly, Frank, let the child have a bit of fun. He's a nice boy and she's growing up.' You know? I can imagine my mother saying all that, but no, not my father. He couldn't bear the idea.

Leonard came to see me. He was outside waiting for me to come out of business one night. And we went home on top of the bus. And he said, 'I want to take you out, go to the pictures together, or go to a dance or something. Why can't you do that?' So I said, 'Well, you'd better ask dad.' So in he came. Dad looked at him very askance. Well Leonard said, 'Oh Mr Butler, I've come to ask if I can take Mary out some times.' Dad was very quiet and then he said, 'Young man, come into the next room with me for a minute.' So they went into the next room and after a few moments I heard the front door bang. Dad came back and said, 'I have told Leonard that you are far too young to start any of this sort of thing. And I want you to know' – looking me very straight in the face – 'that all your kisses are mine, for a very long time to come.'

And that was the end of that. Until the middle of the war, after cousin Ned had been killed. Len thought he would make one more try, I suppose. He came one night, a pouring wet night. I'd got a streaming cold. I was feeling absolutely awful, and I'm sure looking my utter worst, in a grey velvet jumper, trimmed with black around my neck. Anyway in he came, looking by this time absolutely marvellous in officer's uniform. It was dreadful because he was hardly asked to sit down, let alone offered a drink or anything. And at last the boy, not knowing what to do I suppose, said, 'Well I'm afraid I must be going now,' and got up. And dad got up; I made to get up, but didn't exactly, and dad just showed him out of the front door. I was not allowed to be with him for one moment. I've thought about it – oh I did think about it afterwards: if only I could have told Len, just told him – 'Len, I do still love you' – because I did in my heart. But he went and I don't blame him in the slightest because what could he do in such circumstances?

None of my generation was married. There was no one left for us to marry. We were known really as the lost generation. The war ruined everything. Pray for peace whatever you do; war ruins everything. There was the most violent recruiting in the First World War; men at every street corner saying, 'Your king and country need you', stirring up all the young men. One lunch time, out goes Ned. The next thing, he'd said he was older than he was, and he was in uniform and off he went: to France, the trenches, and the Somme. They said he was looking out over the top and telling his friend the names of the wild flowers growing in no man's land – the stretch of land between the English and the Germans. And then the order came, to rush across it killing each other in the middle. And Ned had only been a few yards, a few steps almost, out of the trench, when he was killed instantly. And how I know about the wild flowers was because the friend that was standing next to him survived to come on leave. He went to see my auntie, Ned's mother, and told her: 'Dear old Ned, the last thing he said was telling us the names of the wild flowers.' Yes, truly the virgin soldiers.

Lost Generation

Think of us, of the lost generation
Brought about by the horrors of war.
Think of the millions of husbands
                    and lovers
Snatched to its hungry maw.

Think of the girls who were never mothers
Tho' they longed for a babe in their arms –
Never to know the clasp of a lover
On their wedding day, and 'goodbye
                    to Mother'.

So they picked up the threads
And packed away
Thoughts of a life that is bright and gay.
And set to work to make what they could
Of the life before them,
And made it good.

So think of those of the lost generation
And pray against war
And it's cruel devastation.

                    Mary Butler

*Above right: Mary, aged twenty-six, when
she was working at Bedales School.
Right: Mary's father Frank, a profound
influence on her life after his wife died
when Mary was five weeks old.
Above: Mary's recent poem about the
'million superfluous women' destined
to remain single after the carnage of
the First World War.*

So I went on for quite a time, just sort of more or less doing nothing. But it was understood that Mary could sew very nicely, and all of a sudden somebody in business said to him, 'Oh Mr Butler, you've got a daughter. Would she like to be a milliner do you think? Because if you think so, there's an opening for her at Dickins and Jones.' And so dad, rather put out because I wasn't going to be a showroom lady, rather reluctantly, not knowing what he was going to do with me, said I could do it.

Well, I adored being a milliner. Yes, I really did like it. It was a great change for me. Can you imagine Ascot coming on and how we all would work like mad on these wonderful confections? We made the most marvellous hats for all the aristocracy and actresses of the time. I remember particularly one, and that was Fay Compton. She was the most beautiful girl, wonderful golden hair, and I made her a most wonderful black tulle hat.

All of a sudden my aunt in the country fell and broke her leg. Slipped on a mat, on a polished floor, and so a letter came from a friend of hers. Dad opened it at the breakfast table, and he says, 'Good heavens! Kitty has broken her leg.' Turned to me and said, 'Mary, you must go immediately.' So I said, 'What about business?' 'Oh, can't worry about that.' You see it shows how little he thought of it really. Well, I felt terrible. I was at the top of my profession by this time; I wasn't the designer but I would have gone on to be a designer. I know in my heart I would have done.

In these days aunt would have gone to hospital straight away, but I had to go. The doctor said to me, 'She won't last very long, at her age.' But Aunty lived for many, many years. She came to live with us afterwards. I practically had a breakdown, I really did. I had that wretched sort of breakdown where you cried all the time. I couldn't stop crying, the tears were always running down my face. I wanted a career. I wanted something that was mine. I wanted to earn something and I wanted to get away from home. I really did. I knew in my heart it would hurt dad, but then, I desperately wanted to get away from home.

I eventually got back to London. Well, I couldn't go back to being a milliner, my job had been filled. It was then that I really started to look after children. I desperately wanted a bit of independence, you see. And suddenly I saw an advertisement: 'Wanted. A lady to look after a little girl two or three times a week.' I leapt at it! And went to the most delightful people. She was an adorable child, absolutely. They moved, of course, eventually.

It just so happened that a relation of the lady who lived next door was matron of the junior school at Bedales School. She was wanting to retire and it was suggested that I might go there, to work into her job. I longed to do it, so down I went. I was interviewed and it was settled that I went the next term. Well, then the under-matron, she had to go and look after her sick mother. So a frantic telegram was sent to me, saying could I possibly come at once? Everything I had was flung into a trunk and off I went.

I had the most wonderful time. Because I adore children and children love me too. I used to do walks and tell them stories all the time, tell them the name of the wild flowers and tell them what the trees were. They absolutely loved it and I had a wonderful term. Back I went in the spring term after Christmas. And the children went down with whooping cough. I had never had whooping cough as a child. So I caught it. And the matron got a niece of hers to fill my place, and that was the end of me. I did feel wretched about the Bedales affair because for me it was a time of bliss, happiness; imagine the unimaginable! I adored it! I loved being with those children and I loved the place.

I was going to get another job of that sort. As a matron in a school, that's what I felt I was fitted for. I was sitting there, about to answer a letter that had come from some establishment, and dad sat behind his paper, taking no notice of me at all. I looked down and said, 'Dad, you don't want me to do this do you?' And he said, 'You know I don't.' So I put everything away and forgot it.

I was all he'd got, you see. I mean, one's got to remember he never got over my mother's death. I said to him once, 'Didn't you wish I'd died at the same time?' And he said, 'No! No! Never! Never! I couldn't have borne to have lost everything.' And that tells you an awful lot about how he felt. As I grow older, I think about his character and, you know, I'm sure there was jealousy at the back of it somewhere.

I was thinking the other day, in those days, birth and death and everything all went on around you, in the home. I was with the aunt when she breathed her last. And it was just after that, that my father had a cerebral haemorrhage. He didn't even know me, which was terrible. He thought I was a young man. It was all the more dreadful because the Second World War came upon us then. He'd no idea what was going on. He used to say, 'What's all that noise? What's all that noise?' And it was a battle going on over our heads! I had to bath him, I had to get him into the bath, dress him, take him to the lavatory, do everything, because he didn't know what he was doing. But if things like that happen, you know, you've jolly well got to brace yourself and get on with it. You really have. Or else you just go under, and they do too.

His funeral was too distressing for words. There was a grave in Willesden cemetery which he had bought for my mother, himself, and eventually me, but things don't work out that way. There'd been an appalling raid the night before and when we'd got there, the gravestones were flung about everywhere and there was a huge crater right by the side of the grave. Dreadful. Came back to the house, and the whole thing had been boarded up – I had workmen come up in the morning. The house was completely dark.

I'd had nothing to eat, and I was in a state of the most great distress, as you can imagine. A friend of mine had gone and got something, fish and chips as a matter of fact, but I couldn't eat anything. There was some port wine that was in the house and I put in out on the table and said, 'Oh, just help yourselves.' I was thirsty, distressed, tired and everything else, so I drank this port and when I got up I realised that I was drunk. I had to lie down. And I remember thinking, 'Well if this is getting drunk, why anybody gets drunk to cheer themselves up, I don't know.'

After my father died I was sort of, how shall I put it, free to develop a relationship with someone. I could have hopped into bed with a good number of married men, but that wasn't me. I would never have been happy doing that sort of thing. But I did have a fair amount of difficulty beating off married men. But, in a sort of way, you know every woman – doesn't want to feel that she's completely unattractive to the opposite sex does she?

I'm just the sort of woman who wanted to have children and be somebody's mum. I would have loved to have been married and had an ordinary married existence. I didn't want for much, but I would have liked to have somebody to love me, and children round me that I could love. Of course I would. Yes.

Mary lives by herself in Hampstead Garden Suburb, London, in a house she bought after her father died. She continued to care for older people and children. She also became involved in the work of the Metropolitan Society for the Blind. She collects exotic hats, and she continues to write: autobiography and poetry.

•

JOYCE WILKINS *was born in Derbyshire in 1902. She had an elder sister and a brother, who died before she was born. Her parents were Baptist missionaries and she was taken out to India when she was nine months old. At the age of six she was brought back to England to go with her sister to a school for missionaries' daughters, and was later joined by her younger sister and brother. Joyce did not see her father for nine years.*

The parents had the call and they made a big sacrifice; they went out to preach to the heathen. But the sacrifice was also of the children.

The day after my seventh birthday in January, father and mother went back to India and I remember it so very clearly. We knew they

were going but it was a very traumatic experience. We went to Sevenoaks station to see them off and of course being missionaries, the station was packed with all the congregation of the Baptist church. They sang hymns and prayed and so on, and we two little girls stood by and listened to it all. When the hymns and prayers were over, mother and father kissed us, picked up Eric the baby and Phyllis, and walked along and got into the railway carriage. The guard blew the whistle, slammed the door, and the train moved slowly out. And it struck me then, tremendously forcibly, 'They're going out and leaving me behind.' So much so, that I can remember it even if I go through Sevenoaks station now, I get the feeling of it. Of course I knew they were going, in a way; but I ran after the train as fast as I could, ran the full length of Sevenoaks platform, onto the rough railway track, running after the train, with a porter behind, and Dorothy, my sister, racing to catch me. A very tearful little girl was taken back to school because by then I was a boarder. And that was the beginning of my really traumatic experience.

We wrote letters every week to our parents. My early letters had no conception of the fact that they were so far away. I mean, I would write and say that I was in a play at the end of the term and would they come and see it because I was the Prince. Letter after letter I'd say, 'I hope you're coming to public day', which was quite impossible for them to come from India. We hadn't a guardian like many of the girls had, and we felt very much left out.

When I first went to school I was in the nursery. There was about eight of us, and it was in the hands of a very harsh Nurse Mathieson. I think the people in charge of us were very careful not to be sentimental, not to make a fuss of us, not to make us soft. We'd got to pull up our socks, stop crying and be sensible, you see. The very first night I went there I was crying, and I remember Nurse Mathieson sitting beside me on the bed and going 'boo hoo hoo', making faces. From her point of view, just trying to make this child laugh and stop crying, but from my point of view I felt I was very much abandoned.

Anyway, in the nursery each of us had a washstand that consisted of a large drawer at the bottom for our soiled linen, and then a shelf on which the chamber pot was, and then the top part in which the basin and ewer were. I was seven and I ought to have known better, but I suppose I contemplated this drawer and thought, 'Now if I go in that drawer and pull it shut I could curl up inside.' I mean, any Freudian would say wanting to return to the womb. So I climbed into the bottom drawer of my washstand and of course it tipped up. The basin and ewer broke on my head. There was smashed glass, china, water, everywhere. The nurse came in: 'What on earth do you think you were doing?' Well, a child can't explain that I thought I could get in that drawer and close it around me. So I was scolded tremendously. But worse than that, the story was told to the headmistress, who whenever she met me, especially if she'd got visitors, said, 'What do you think this funny little girl did the other day? She climbed into her dirty linen drawer.' Well, you see, put like that it's very different from the idea of trying to hide yourself in a deep drawer. There were lots of upsetting incidents like that.

The chief difficulty was, in common parlance now you'd say I was dyslexic. I couldn't relate sound to symbol and I couldn't write correctly. Therefore I was branded as more stupid than I really was. Also, I never had a full term without being ill. I was at the cottage, that is the sanatorium, for part of every term and therefore missed so much schooling that when I got back I didn't know what was going on.

I sort of day-dreamed instead of trying to catch up and I remember full well one of the mistresses, when I was in the first form after having moved in from the kindergarten, saying, 'What's the matter with you Joycie, you're walking about like a lost soul.' Well now, that doesn't mean anything very much to most people, but to a missionary's daughter a 'lost soul' was beyond the pale. If you were a lost soul you were absolutely lost! So I had the feeling definitely that I was a lost soul.

You had to kneel by your bed and say your prayers, and it was all that kind of puritan background which gave one a great sense of guilt. My friends said they'd seen angels; and I thought, 'Well I'm not good enough to see an angel.' And they said, 'Oh I saw an angel in the corner of my bedroom.' 'Oh well, you're lucky,' I thought. I couldn't see an angel; no angel would come and see me.

When the headmistress thought it was about time we should know the facts of life, she would send for us one at a time, and you'd sit down and she'd say, 'I want to tell you about things.' I remember sitting on the end of the sofa, tears streaming down my cheeks because it was such a solemn occasion. She sat in an armchair opposite and started to tell me very solemnly about menstruation, about the womb bleeding, and making a nest for the baby, and so on. But I got very confused about it all and I thought that this happened for nine months. And she kept saying you must be very sweet and very kind and very nice, and you'll feel miserable but you mustn't show that. So I thought that throughout the nine months I would be a model mum, do everything that she told me, and there I sat weeping silently while she told me about it. But I didn't realise that she was telling me of menstruation that was going to be once a month. And when I found that out, I thought this was really more than I'd bargained for!

Also I remember quite clearly feeling when I was highly depressed that I could never bear to have a child because I could never bear a child of mine to suffer as I was suffering, who might be as miserable as me. I really resigned myself in adolescence not to have a child. So then when I was grown up and I would have liked to have had somebody fall in love with me, I suppose I never gave out the right signals. I was much too shy, and withdrawn, and difficult.

On leaving school I was reading a book on careers for women and in one chapter a name was mentioned: Elsie Fogerty of the Central School of Speech Training and Dramatic Art, Royal Albert Hall, Kensington. She said that she had training for the stage students, and training for teachers of, I don't think she said elocution, I think she would say 'diction'. And she said also, 'Stammering can be treated and cleft palate speech corrected.' I had a friend at school who was a stammerer. And I was tongued as a child and I remember it being cut, very unpleasant. So I thought, 'That's what I want to do.' So I got father's permission to go and see Miss Fogerty, even though he was very concerned because as a strict Nonconformist he'd never been to a theatre – he didn't approve of theatres. Later we took him to see a play, and he bowed in prayer at the beginning and we said, 'Shhh, you mustn't do that in the theatre', and he said, 'If I'm not allowed to pray here, I won't stay.'

Anyway, after I'd done a year, phonetics, anatomy and physiology and voice, I went to India for four years. I taught for a year in a school and tried to run a correspondence course for stammerers, which was not very successful financially, but I hope I gave a few stammerers some ideas that might be helpful. But I got more and more depressed and more and more unhappy. You see, I'd been separated from them so much that we were strangers really. Mother wasn't an affectionate person, she never

Joyce, aged eighteen, on her father's left, on the occasion of her parents' Silver Wedding Anniversary. Her brother Eric is on her father's right and in the front row is her mother with sisters Dorothy and Phyllis.

put her arms around you, she'd never hug you or make a fuss. I used to say to her, 'When was the happiest time of your life?' 'What a silly thing to say dear, how do I know?' That kind of thing, you see?

Father was much more affectionate but he didn't understand us. He used to comment, and presumably when I was born, that children ought to be born three years old because they're no use to their father before then. Very different from now when fathers are even present at the birth, and feel a sense of responsibility for their children all the way through. But the Victorian father didn't feel like that. It wasn't just my parents; the Victorian father had nothing to do with the nursery or the children when they were little.

And we were always feeling that the daughters were not very important but my brother was. Enormously important. To carry on the name. And in the case of my brother, he did go as a missionary: he carried on the tradition as well, which made him doubly valuable to my parents.

When we came back to this country in 1926 I simply was at home with my parents. I was the housekeeper and did all the cooking and the shopping, running the family home, looking after my parents. My life was being wasted. And I felt I couldn't do anything more than that. And then I decided – my sister Dorothy was a psychiatrist, so analysis was quite a reasonable thing in our family, unlike perhaps in other families – I decided I must have an analysis. Which I did: not a very complete one, but one lasting about nine months, five times a week – pretty severe.

When I was offered a job, in Nottingham, I left home and went up there. Because that made it possible: without the analysis I certainly couldn't have. I remember at the end of the analysis saying to the doctor as I went out, 'I shall get married now.' And she said, 'Don't be so sure.' She was objecting to my making a definite stipulation. And that sort of made me feel, 'Oh well, perhaps I shan't after all.' I felt I'd got to the stage where I could get married; I'd got rid of all my anxieties, or a lot of my anxieties and fears and so on. But the way she said 'Well don't be so sure' rather shattered my confidence.

It would have been marvellous to have had children, to have been picked out, loved enough to be asked to marry somebody. But nobody ever did. I probably never sent the right signals out. We didn't expect to get married because we were the result of the First World War – the one million superfluous women they spoke about. And the education that we had, at school it was implied that it was your duty to use your learning for the benefit of the world.

You have 'Dateline' nowadays and I read the adverts and think, 'Well fancy that.' But I did once (I wonder how old I was? Thirtyish or a bit more) send for one of these things, you know, in the plain envelope on how to attract men. I was so disgusted when I read it, with all the things that I was supposed to do, I just sat and laughed. But you know I paid thirty shillings or something, for all this so-called information.

Mother of course was very funny: if a young man talked to us, mother always managed to come between us. If we were coming out of church and were talking to a young man, mother would come along and sort of wedge herself in. We used to laugh about it.

I should have loved to have had children. I think one goes through a stage where it is terribly frustrating that you have nobody to pass on to the next generation. As you get older you get more reconciled, more resigned, but in middle age it's very difficult. You're still really alive, physically, and wanting children. You feel you've lost out on something, which should be everybody's experience.

I would have loved to have found somebody, but, no, I never really have. You could burst into tears when you hear a tune such as 'Some enchanted evening, you will see a stranger'. One always hoped to see a stranger, find somebody on holiday, somewhere. You went off, hopeful that you might, but of course you never did.

Joyce worked as a pioneer speech therapist from the 1930s, first for the London County Council, then as a university and community lecturer in Nottingham. She retired at sixty and now lives in sheltered accommodation in Sussex, where she regularly attends her keep fit classes. She has published a book on her early childhood.

•

DOROTHY GALTON *was born in Hornsey, North London, in 1902, and, like Mary and Joyce, she was greatly influenced by her parents' attitudes, but whereas they, by their own accounts, were restricted and handicapped by their parents' actions, Dorothy found freedom.*

Her mother had been a teacher and her father was an apprentice engraver for a London goldsmith's before becoming a political journalist and later, between the wars, secretary to the Fabian Society. She had a sister, Joan, two years older than herself and they were brought up in a non-religious home which embraced the Socialist creed of many intellectuals of that time. Dorothy remembers sitting through 'rather boring dinners with Sidney and Beatrice Webb'. From an early age she was encouraged by her parents to be independent-minded.

I think that the person who greatly influenced my father and mother was probably William Morris who was an artist and designer of all kinds of furniture, hangings, tapestries – he revived the medieval way of preparing these things. And he saw how everything connected and his philosophy – his unified system of thought – ran through everything. It gave you your principles, your attitude to other people, which you always tried to live up to if you could. You didn't squabble, you treated people as human beings and not as lumps of muck, and generally tried to be as decent as possible. This kind of attitude must have been fairly common among the semi-intellectuals in those days and because my father was an apprentice in one of the famous goldsmith's in London as an engraver, he got into artistic circles and from there into political circles as well.

My father came in touch with the Webbs, Sidney and Beatrice, and he joined the Social Democratic Federation and did street lectures, public speaking and all this kind of thing. He was often out at nights, in fact almost every night of the week, and it used to be a certain worry to me, I remember. I used to find it difficult to go to sleep until I heard he'd come home. So I wasn't used to going to sleep until about midnight every night, which wasn't perhaps good, but it didn't seem to affect me. My sister and I rarely saw him except at weekends, because he had his dinner with my mother while we were doing homework or otherwise engaged, and then he would go out again. And so it was mostly weekends and holidays when we saw him. I think my father's political stance influenced us all very much and that it permeated our household. A general atmosphere. It was never thrust down our throats or anything but it was there; we lived among it, and I think that was the major influence in my life.

One of the great moments in the life of our family was the Russian Revolution in 1917. My father got very excited and we all stood up and cheered, because it was a Socialist revolution as we thought. It wasn't just our family, there was great excitement everywhere – people thought the world was going to change. Dad talked about that all during the First World War – the world was going to change; it was going to be new afterwards. Of course it never was in our country. We thought that the Russians were going to do it, and they did. The changes that were made in Russia were simply enormous and you couldn't avoid seeing them if you went there. Some of it went very wrong, as we later learned. It makes you very unhappy. But it led me to read Marx and to understand his philosophy in connection with my background and many other things.

From my point of view and for people of my generation and upbringing and beliefs, the modern situation is absolutely appalling. Everybody says that Socialism is dead, and it isn't of course. We know it isn't! It's a whole life's work, a whole life's beliefs down the drain. They talk like that and the world now, under the present government, is going back to Victorian times. It's not what we ought to be doing; it's dirty and nasty, and is something that we ought to be fighting – everybody ought to fight it. However, they don't – and it can be very depressing if you think about it.

During the First World War, Middlesex County Council didn't have enough pupils to form both boys' and girls' secondary schools and they were running joint mixed schools. I went to this mixed school and, having no brothers, it impressed me. I found it agreeable. We were all pals together, so at the school I had as my friends Duncan and Willy. We

Dorothy, centre, aged five, with her mother and elder sister Joan.

used to go out to the library that was open until nine o'clock at night. Our parents didn't like us going out very much: it was dark, no lights, and there might be a Zeppelin raid or something. But on the whole my parents were very free and they didn't worry. We used to meet at the library and have a little walk and so on but nothing happened. We never even kissed, never even kissed.

When I got to Bedford College, which was women only, I found it absolutely appalling. They were mostly rather upper-class girls, very opposed to my general outlook, or rather I was opposed to their general outlook I should say, and it really was a miserable time. I couldn't stand it. My work went down, I couldn't do my studies properly, and everything went wrong. I don't know whether there were other people in the same boat but that was my reason for leaving. My father was angry of course. He said, 'Oh no you mustn't' and so on, but I did and that was it. He took it eventually, but I think he was always rather annoyed I didn't finish.

Then of course I had to find a job because my father's principles were that you had to stand on your own feet and I didn't like being dependent upon my parents. You see women were in the home in those days and very much subjected to home life and to the husband's or father's finances. I know my mother didn't have a bank account. She did not share one with my father and that was typical of this kind of middle class (rather lower than upper) that I belonged to. I could see, from her life, that she was purely dependent. She had done some teaching before she married. She didn't have great means, her father wasn't very well off, she didn't earn anything, so naturally she was dependent upon my father. I suppose my father gave her an allowance of some sort but it was only doled out; it wasn't an account she could use on her own when she wanted special things, children's clothes or whatnot. She had to ask for it or skimp her housekeeping money in order to buy something. I found that appalling. I saw it from an early age, and I thought that was all wrong and that it should be altered.

In my later life I was determined to be independent and look after myself and have my own bank account and such like. Even when I went to college my father received my scholarship, not me! We didn't have bank accounts like young people do today and if I wanted anything, bus fares or pocket money, I had to ask for it and it was very difficult sometimes.

So I found a job, strangely enough in the Labour Party Head Office. I was there from about 1919 to '22 or '3, I suppose, and in the course of working there I met these Hungarians, Michael and Catherine Karolyi. He had been the Socialist President of Hungary in 1917 when Hungary broke away from Austria during the First World War, but he only lasted a few months because he was ousted, and he became an émigré with his family. Eventually they came to England and as they were Socialists it was natural for them to come to the Labour Party. After a time, they asked me whether I would go to Paris with them as their assistant and secretary, which I did. That was the great time in Paris: the artistic crowd were all there. We were in the Left Bank part of the time and the summer at Deauville, a very fashionable racecourse place. Still is. I spent nearly two years in Paris. In the course of which I fell ill.

I suddenly found this very severe pain in my left knee and I hopped and hobbled about and eventually went to a Polish doctor, woman doctor, who said it was probably water on the knee. The treatment she gave me was to burn spots on the knee with a white-hot platinum rod. It was rather painful and it didn't do any good. Then I found a specialist of some sort who took lots of X-rays, and his judgement was TB, so then something had to be done. My parents wouldn't have been able to afford this on their own but joining forces with various friends and all sorts of relatives we raised a considerable sum of money and so I was able to go to this private sanatorium. I was transported by sleeper train from Paris to a place below the mountains in Switzerland and then a taxi or an ambulance up the hill. It was autumn and the trees were beautiful, and I remember feeling as we went up this hill, 'Ah! this is the place, I'll be well.'

I was very much alone in my room. I had a beautiful view and I was in circumstances that I enjoyed and which suited me. I was able to think and do things on my own, in my own time, as best I could from the confines of my bed. I think it was a very informative time for me and it made a big effect because now I can easily be alone without worrying. All my life it hasn't worried me and so it suited my way of thinking, my way of life. As I had made up my mind in childhood almost that I wasn't going to get married, I knew I would have a lot of time alone, and that was all right.

I had a philosophy about this, you see. It was my mother's experience mostly, and what I saw going on around me, other people's houses. I wasn't going to run a bourgeois house. I hadn't the slightest intention of doing such a thing and never did, never did at all. Right back in the early twenties, before I went away with the Karolyis, I met an older man at the Young Fabians. He had been in the war and we started walking about together, night after night, at the Queen's Hall, walking a bit in London and so on. Well yes, we did have an affair and eventually it came to an end, partly because I went abroad. When I came back to England I called on him again and I thought, 'My God! Is this the man?!' You see, by that time I had altered my attitude to things altogether and it just seemed impossible. So that was the end of that – very much so!

But I have to confess that I knew men were attracted to me rather and I loved talking to them. I had many men friends with whom I had long, long conversations but I purposely didn't do anything flashy to egg them on. I didn't wear flashy clothes, I didn't wear jewellery, I carefully kept myself in the background, if you see what I mean, because I knew that it wasn't wise to encourage them too much if I wasn't going to be serious. The men I knew were nearly all intellectual sort of people and they understood. They knew if asked I would say no and so they didn't bother to ask. Quite rightly.

I had been abroad four years – this was 1928 – and when I came back I had a short rest and then looked for a job. I put my name down with an organisation called The Ladies League, frightfully posh, they found you jobs. They sent me to a City firm, a bank I think it was, for translation, and of course I didn't know anything about French banking. Then they sent me to those people who look after feet, you know – Scholl. Oh there was going to be a brilliant future for me in Scholl but I had to start by working in the shop. As I hated feet I said I couldn't do that, so I turned that away, and finally, much to my pleasure, I was invited to go and see Sir Bernard Pears, who was Professor of Russian Studies at King's College in London. He and I got on like wild fire and so he appointed me as his private secretary. He was very liberal in his outlook, not a Socialist by any means, but liberal. He generally believed in women working and women's rights, and he was a person whose views I could appreciate. I stayed with him until my retirement.

Once a week, as a change from my daily work I used to go and help at a birth control clinic in the East End of London. We had to say to the women, as they left, 'Before you use the appliance you've been given, it would be wise if your husband used ... what we then called a French letter, which is a condom of course ... Do you think he will need a large one or a small one?' They got very embarrassed at this and very often couldn't answer, so we did what we thought best and gave them a large one! And they went away, again rather shamefacedly. They were all so embarrassed by the whole situation, because it was so unusual, so new.

The private doctor who ran the clinic would give anybody contraceptive advice, including me of course, but those doctors were few and far between, and you were jolly lucky to find one if you were single. They were often on the left so we did know quite a number of them.

Most people didn't know anything about it – they were quite ignorant, quite ignorant. I told one or two women about this clinic and they had no idea there were such things – nothing at all. It was not a subject that anybody talked about. They weren't interested in these activities; in fact, everybody was a bit shamefaced about sexual activity in those days, very – diffident in talking about such things.

In the thirties I had one major affair which was very important to me because it was again with somebody whose philosophical outlook was similar to mine at that time. I found it a most rewarding experience that has lasted all my life actually. He had the same sense of needing room and freedom and space and that sort of thing, and it was that that appealed to me I think. I always wanted to be myself. I didn't want interference. I didn't want to have to necessarily comply with things I didn't approve of or didn't want. That was my attitude. It probably is selfish but I can't help that. I've always wanted space, room, air, freedom, and the idea of being tied up with somebody always seemed absolutely impossible to me and always has done.

I hope I was an emancipated woman. That's what I tried to be but I don't know whether I succeeded. I think I did. Most people who know me would say so, I think. Yes. I don't regret anything. I'm happy as a sandboy about my life as far as I can be. I'm not complacent about it but I feel I've done what I meant it to do.

After retiring at sixty, Dorothy became secretary of the Hertfordshire Beekeepers' Association. Later she moved to Norfolk but still remained active in the Labour Party, which recently awarded her a medal in recognition of all her work over the years. She was writing a book on the history of bees when she died in the summer of 1992.

6 *Pennies on their Eyes*

T alking about death is harder than talking about sex for many people today: especially for the young, who are least likely to have experienced death. When our ninety-year-olds were young it was the reverse. Sex was the unspoken secret, but death was part of common experience. This was partly because, unlike today, death at most ages was still quite common, and especially in early childhood, rather than only in later years. So most people grew up knowing from early experience what it was like to lose a loved one: a brother or sister, a parent or a friend. Loss from death was familiar. You learnt early how to grieve – and how life had to go on. Many ninety-year-olds can still look death square in the face now, nearing the end of their own lives.

There has been a profound change in the public ceremony of death. Even if the ostentatious pomp of Victorian funerals was beginning to fade by the early years of the century, a decent send-off was regarded as essential for any respectable family. Among the working classes, the most widespread form of insurance was to pay for funerals. A pauper's burial – a plain box in an unmarked grave – was a shame to be avoided if at all possible.

A funeral might be public, but death itself was centred on the neighbourhood and the home. After someone died, the body would be laid out in the home by a local handywoman, like Rose Ashton, one of our contributors. Neighbours and children would come in to see. In some parts of the country they would watch over the body day and night in a wake.

The mass carnage of young men in the First World War, as witnessed by Norman Collins as a burial officer at the Somme, made it difficult to sustain the public celebration of death back at home in the old style. The shock at the unexpected loss of so many young lives was one reason for the subtle change in people's attitudes towards death from the twenties onwards. The introduction of funeral parlours and the increase of cremations over traditional burials saw death taken out of the home and professionally distanced. It became stranger, and perhaps more frightening: for many, today's unspoken secret.

ROSE ASHTON *was born in Dudley, in the Midlands, in 1893. When she was five years old, she moved with her parents and her three brothers and two sisters to Barrow-in-Furness in Cumbria. Her father had found a job as a caretaker in a foundry, and they lived in a cottage that belonged to the works. Her mother added to their income by doing cleaning work in the evenings. Rose was very close to both her parents. But life was a struggle. At fourteen she left school and went into service, mostly in Barrow. But she got her first job on a farm, by going to the hiring fair in nearby Ulverston.*

We went at November, 11th November was hiring day, and as me mam couldn't afford to give us the money so we walked, me and my friend. All the farmers used to walk up and down King Street and they used to come to us and they'd say, 'Ist thee for hiring lass?' and we used to say, 'Yes.' 'Can you do this? Can you wash? Can you bake?' 'Yes.' Then we used to say, 'What are you going to give us?' 'Oh, we'll give you six pounds.' That's the way they used to talk. 'Oh no,' we would say, 'not six pounds for six months. No.' And we used to leave him. Then we used to walk on and meet another farmer. 'Ist thee for hiring lass?' 'Yes.' He'd ask us the same question. 'And what are you going to give us?' 'We'll give thee five pounds.' 'Oh no.'

The hiring day was over at twelve o'clock and if you didn't get hired before twelve o'clock you were finished. When it got nearly to twelve o'clock we met this farmer. 'Ist thee for hiring?' 'Yes.' 'And what you going to give us?' 'I'll give you six pounds ten shillings.' 'Right.' Accepted! You got a silver shilling then. Now that silver shilling bound you to go to them for six months. If you failed to go, your parents had to pay the six pounds money back. We used to spend that silver shilling, have a cup of tea and a bun, and then we used to get on the bus and come back home.

When I was in farm service, it was Christmas time, so this was my first Christmas away from home. We had a lovely Christmas dinner. They were very kind to me, very kind. I washed up and I'd done all the sides and cleaned all me back up, and she came into me, she says, 'Have you finished Rose?' And I said, 'Yes, madam.' She said, 'Well I want you to go down to the paddock.' Now the paddock was the toilet. It was a good way down from the farmyard and it had two wooden seats, one on each side so two could get on the toilet at once. So she said, 'See that roll of paper there?' And I said, 'Yes madam.' And she said, 'Well, here's a ball of string and here's a big needle. I want you to go down the paddock and tear this paper into pieces and thread them with this string and hang it on the back of the toilet door.' Well I went down the paddock, I took this paper, took the string, tore this paper into little pieces, threaded it through and hung it on the back of the toilet door. I cried all the while. I cried all the while for thinking about me mam and dad having a nice Christmas, and me sitting on a toilet seat. The farm was at Longridge – I only went once, I never went no more.

One day, mother was getting fat and we didn't know a thing. We was as innocent as dew. We were going to bed one night and we could hear this tramping up and down the stairs and I said to my sister, 'Mammy must be bad, I'm going to get out of bed.' And my sister said, 'Get back, our Rose, it'll be all right.' I said, 'I'm going to get out of bed.' I got out of bed and me dad was on the landing. I said, 'Dad, what's the matter? Is mam bad?' He said, 'Your mam's bad, but she'll be better in the morning, me lass. Go on, get back to bed.' So I got back to bed.

I got up the next morning, went in the bedroom. I said, 'Have you been bad, mam?' She said, 'Yes lass.' I said, 'What been the matter with you?' She said, 'Well, look on the washstand' – there were washstands in those days – 'you'll see a pillow and you'll see a baby on there.' 'A baby? Where's that come from?' 'Now,' she said, 'ask no questions and you'll get no lies. Just lift the handkerchief up and have a look at it.' I lifted the handkerchief up and – it was like a little doll! It wasn't full born, it was dead; and it had this handkerchief over it. 'Now,' she said, 'you weren't to go to school today, Rose.' 'Oh,' I said, 'why mam?' She said,

'Your daddy's left a letter and you've got to do a bit of business for your daddy. Now the first thing,' she said, 'I want you to go to the fruit shop and ask for a soap box.' 'A soap box, mam? What do you want a soap box for?' 'To bury it in,' she said.

Now in those days soap boxes was like a Tupper box – it had no nails in – just press down. On my way to the shop I called to my friend in the next street. I said to Bessie, 'My mam's got a baby.' She says, 'Has she?' I said, 'Yes! and oh! it's like a little doll. It's beautiful, Bessie.' She said, 'I'll come round with you.' 'Oh,' I said, 'I'm going for a soap box first, Bessie.'

So we went and got the soap box, only small, and I took the soap box back to mam, took it upstairs. She said, 'Just bring that pillow to me.' 'You can't put that baby in this box, mam,' I said. So my friend Bessie said, 'Have you some wadding?' And she says, 'We've plenty of wadding.' We said, 'Well, give us the wadding mam and we'll go downstairs with the soap box.' Me and Bessie lined this little soap box with the wadding, took it back up to mam, took this pillow, give mam it. Mam put the little baby in this box. It was very small, just a doll, just a doll. So I said, 'Oh, don't put the lid on, we're going put some wadding over its face.' We put some wadding over its face. 'Now,' she said, 'put the lid on it.' Then mam said, 'Now you've got to go up the cemetery.' 'Oh,' I said, 'We can't go to the cemetery now with that under our arms.' So I came downstairs and I went underneath the stairs and dad had an old coat under there. We tore the black lining out of dad's old coat and me and Bessie wrapped this little box up in this black lining and tied it up with string.

Off we went up the cemetery with the baby under our arms and the letter. 'You've got to give it to the first grave-digger you see.' 'Right.' Went up the cemetery, saw a grave-digger. 'Say mister, me daddy sent you this.' He read the letter. 'Oh yes, me lass,' he said, 'it's quite alright. You see the church over there, by the corner?' We said, 'Yes.' He said, 'Well in that corner you'll find a lot of parcels.' Bessie and I went and we were surprised to see all these boxes and parcels and bundles. Inquisitive Rose went back to the grave-digger, said to him, 'Mister, what do you do with all those parcels up there?' He said, 'Well you see, me lass, people haven't got the money to buy graves these days. So,' he said, 'when the grave gets full up we put one of those parcels at the top and one at the bottom.' 'Oh,' I said, 'that's what you do with them is it?' He says, 'Yes, you're alright, me lass. They're put in and we get rid of them.'

Oh we cried, we cried we did. We laid it so nice and gently at the foot of all those parcels that was there. They were too young to be buried like paupers. When we got back, mam was pleased we'd done that and when dad come in from work he said we'd done a good day's work. And that was the end of it.

Later on, I used to help in the neighbourhood if an adult died. Well, the first thing you done was to take the fire out of the bedroom; they used to have fires in the bedroom in those days to keep them warm. You'd wash 'em, sponged them right down; and put her straight; straight, not crimped; put her arms well down, hands just crossed or by her side, so they would set. If her mouth opened and you couldn't shut it, you got a handkerchief and you tied it up the top until it set, then you would take it off after. If her eyes wouldn't close you would put a bit of tape on the cheek and put a penny on it till it closed, and you'd take it off later. You took all the bedding away, put a clean sheet on, laid her out on the sheet and covered her up ready for the undertaker. You'd come down, you would tell the lady or whoever it was, would she like to go up to see it. You'd take her up to see and you would bring her down. You would put your arms around her. You'd try and comfort them and if it was a man or woman that had suffered, you'd just got to say, 'Well love, they're better off. You wouldn't like them to live and suffer all their life like this.' You would have a cup of tea and she would thank you. That would be your good deed for the day. You never received any money because you done that as a favour.

My children, getting them ready for school, they said to me, 'Who was that knocking the door mam?' 'Oh, it was Mrs So and So, she died.' 'Oh yes? Well, what did she want you for?' I said, 'Well, I go and wash them and lay them out.' 'Oh, that's what you do is it?' I said, 'Yes. Now come get ready for school.' She said, 'You know what I would do mam?' I said, 'I know what I would do with you if you don't get ready!' She said, 'I'd put a card in the window – "laying out taken in".' She said, 'They're always knocking you up.' I said, 'Well, that's the only thing you can do – help one another.'

Neither a mother, or husband nor wife wouldn't lay anybody out. If she lost her own baby, she couldn't do it. If she lost her husband she couldn't do it. *You* couldn't. You would be too grieved to do it. You're glad of any neighbour coming in and doing that little good deed. You didn't see the undertaker, you didn't see the person after you laid him out. You see nothing, you do nothing, but if you wanted to go to the cemetery you went. If you didn't wish to go you used to say, 'I'm sorry but I'd rather stay at home.'

Everyone in the street would draw the curtains or the blinds, and everybody would give a copper for a few flowers. We used to put it on a chair at the front door – and the bill – so people could see what had been paid for that little wreath. Then they would line up at the door, line up, like a guard of honour, while you walked the coffin down to the hearse. That was their respect; that's what they used to do. We used to come back from the cemetery, to your mother's or a neighbour's next door. A couple of neighbours used to come in the house and you'd get some ham and some cakes, and you'd lay a table and you'd have a tea when you came back.

People would wear all black: black hats, black gloves. The men, black ties and dark-blue suits. A widow could wear a widow's weed; it used to go over the hat like a veil hanging down. Now when I lost my husband I wore black for about two months but after that I just wore the black dress, a working dress. I used to go to the cemetery every Sunday, take a few flowers. But you never forget them, don't matter how long they've been dead, you never forget them. They're still with you, they're still with you. If they're not with you in person they're with you in spirit, right?

Rose had 'two golden husbands'. She met her first husband, a crane driver, when she was working as a barmaid. He died of consumption seven years after they were married, leaving Rose with three young daughters to bring up. Rose lost three other children, two infants and a son at the age of five. She chose a second husband she was sure would be good to the girls. 'I let him court the children, I just let him see how he was going to treat me kiddies.'

She still lives in Barrow, in her own house, a widow once more, yet strongly independent. She is close to her family and very much enjoys cooking for herself and her grandson, who often visits her for lunch. She faces both her centenary celebrations and life's end without fear: 'I'm not afraid, no.'

•

NORBERT BARRY *was born in May 1900 near Newry in Northern Ireland. His father was a sea captain and he remembers his mother being a 'very dainty, very pretty, artistic woman who loved flowers and music'. When Norbert was ten years old, news arrived that his father had been killed on board ship. His mother, left without an income, managed to bring up the six children so that they were well dressed and educated. Norbert was taught by the Dominicans and on leaving school he was asked if he would like to become a priest. Prompted by a spirit of adventure rather than 'spiritual aspirations', he was ordained some years later. Like many Irish children he was no stranger to death, and one of his earliest memories was of attending a wake.*

I was brought by the hand and we went into the house where the wake was, and up the stairs to the room where the corpse was laid out on the bed. People were sitting all around here, all very quiet. I had a look at them, I suppose, but I was more interested in what was in the bed. I went over to the bed and I stood up on my toes to have a look at the figure of the gentleman asleep. He was draped out in a garment they laid on the corpses. I thought the man was sound asleep, but the poor man was

dead: eyes closed, hands joined, and he had rosary beads and a cross
there on his chest, and three candles round the bed.

I wasn't frightened. Children, Irish children, are not one bit frightened
of corpses. Some children would be frightened, but I wasn't frightened.
It was interesting. Children here all gather and follow the hearse going
along the road – entertainment, I suppose, of a type. They seem to love
the funeral. They even go to the graveside, see the grave filled in, looking
into the hole where the corpse was being put down. Irish children are
interested in funerals.

In Ireland, death is taken as one of the unavoidables. In England, it
is pushed not under the carpet exactly, but out of the way. It is referred
to as 'a passing away', to say 'he is at rest', 'gone to God' perhaps. In
England, when you go to party, you don't talk about death. If you do,
you are not invited to the party any more. But in Ireland they don't
mind talking about everything under the sun. More loquacious perhaps,
I don't know. But the outlook seems to be different, completely.

Traditionally, ladies were not allowed to go to the cemetery. It was
an all-male affair. I suppose it was a man's world. Things have changed
a little bit today. They all went to the church. The corpse was brought
to the church and the service was held there by the minister. The ladies
went to the church with the men, but only the men went to the graveside,
down the cemetery. The others chatted and talked and went off home.
That was the funeral.

When there is a tragedy of any kind, particularly in the neighbourhood, they either ring at the door or they come into you and say,
'Would you please call at number so and so.' And you go along. You
have to size up the situation as best you can. If it's a man, you give a
little bit of comfort to them. If it's somebody that is dying you have to
anoint them.

You have patients who are terribly frightened of death when you
go to see them first in their sickness. But as death approaches they are
perfectly serene, perfectly calm and quiet, and take it. Not the least
perturbed. Even some lads who were not exactly gospel greedy, who
were not saying their prayers night, noon or morning, they enjoyed
themselves in this way and that way – even them. When it comes to
death they are amazingly resigned. Surprising.

Normally, you don't stay until they die, unless they are on the point
of death. Sometimes you know more than the doctor himself might know;
your experience teaches you they are on their way out, they will go any
moment. Some have that instinct, some haven't it, I suppose. When you
get word that the patient has deceased, you call back again to give them
your condolences.

The mourners here flock in to give their condolences to people who
are bereaved. They are not all accommodated, naturally, in one room.
They are separated. Some would be in the kitchen, some would be in
the drawing room, some of them would be in the room with the corpse,
the bedroom. There was always refreshments. Some kind of refreshments
were stronger than others, but they were all acceptable. What the ladies
got I'm not too sure. I'd say they got a cup of tea and some confectionery.
The gentlemen got something in a glass and you wouldn't know what
that would be. And if the priest came in he would say 'good afternoon'
to all the people, and then he would go over to the corpse and sprinkle
holy water and say a few prayers. The people would answer him when
he was saying the prayers. Then he would say 'good afternoon' and out
he went. That was the priest's job.

They don't want any advice for the first few days. It's afterwards
the problems arise. One kind or another. They want a little bit of kindness,
and patience and sympathy for the first few days. If you are able to give
them advice, well and good. If you are not, you recommend them to
somebody who is better qualified than yourself.

I remember when my father died in Liverpool on board ship, doing
his job, the boss. Dropped like that. Picked up dead. The man who was
at the wheel of the ship let go of the wheel to pick him up, and the next
thing the ship had crashed – no one was steering. He was brought home
the next morning and I'll never forget to my dying day the sounding of
the ship's horn coming into the harbour and then the corpse coming up

the road into the house. My mother in the back of the house with the youngest child in her arms and her scream! Very, very vivid. It registered there and it will remain there until I am gone too. The homecoming.

She was heartbroken. My mother never went to the graveyard. She never once went to the cemetery. We were sent with flowers, regular, month after month. But she never once went to the graveyard. I think she was afraid of death.

Norbert shortly before being ordained as a priest.

Father Barry taught for a number of years in a Dominican school, where he pursued his love of sport and became the games master and later the head of college. As a priest, he has had to live wherever he has been sent to work. 'I would have loved to have lived at the sea, or on the land, because the land is in me and the sea is in my blood. But it was not to be.'

At over ninety he is still a hive of energy and enthusiasm: he shares the busy duties of the priory at Newry, regularly taking Mass and hearing confession, and every Wednesday he fasts. Philosophical about the ending of his days, he says: 'I'm not one bit afraid of dying. I know very little about the afterlife: nobody has returned to tell us anything about it, that's a fact. If I had to go, that's that.'

•

DAVID WILLIAMSON *was born in the Crumlin Road, Belfast, in 1900. Next door was the family undertaking business, Houston & Williamson. He had three brothers, of whom the eldest went missing in action in the First World War. Only much later, after a terrible time of waiting, was his death confirmed.*

David remembers his mother with much affection; she ran the firm with calm and efficiency. In his youth David, however, had no thought of joining the family profession. He started work as an apprentice in the Belfast shipyards but, like many others, he found himself out of a job once the postwar recession took hold.

After the First World War, everything had gone very flat. I was at that time working in the shipyards, then there was a big lay-off and I was out of work. Whenever I came home I drove the car and looked after any of the motor vehicles that were about the place. Some days you had a car and according to what it was doing, it might come straight off a funeral, get cleaned and then go out to a wedding. Nobody thought anything of

it. If there was a funeral somewhere, I would drive the car and someone else would be driving the hearse. Then I might be asked to go to the hospital and give them a lift: it always took two men to bring a body back. I always remember the first time I felt a body. Cold. It put a shiver up through me. But you see, like anything else, you got sort of seasoned to it. You got used to it.

There was a power of children died. I was looking into some of our old books, from my mother's day. She kept a sort of diary, instead of a ledger, and the funerals are all marked. And if you had sold three funerals, you could put five shillings on that one of them was a child. There was a terrible lot of deaths in those days. The stillborn child; and you had them dying from diphtheria, scarlet fever, all different things. Young girls coming about seventeen dying of tuberculosis; working in the mills, you know, and contracted lung cancer.

In those days, for children up to about five years old, you used a white coffin. But the old, full-sized ones were mostly black, cloth-covered coffins. At the same time you had the polished coffin and anyone that wanted it could have the polished coffin. We would suggest to them what wood we thought was suitable and generally it was always something of a reasonable quality, not the top and not the bottom, but something that we were sure they would be satisfied with. For instance, there was the solid oak coffin with brass mounting: quite expensive. Whereas they could have had an imitation oak with brass handles, which looked quite well. But people, irrespective of price, wanted a black coffin. It was a sort of tradition. Mostly they would have nothing else.

Generally, there was a woman in the district and whenever the death took place or maybe before it took place, they were in touch with her. She was what I would have called a 'handywoman'. Even at a birth she was there. If someone was ill, maybe she would come and sit up with them, you see. So if anything happened they sent for her. She did the dressing and laying out, and we supplied them with what we would have called the 'outfit'.

Now the outfit comprised of a shroud, or a night-dress or shirt, which generally had a dickie-bow on it, see. Along with that you would supply them with stockings and gloves and a veil. Then you would probably lend them a couple of pillow slips, a bolster, a sheet, a bedspread and then a couple more because they probably would want to drape the ends of the bed. They would tie a fine bit of ribbon round the knobs of the bed. They always pulled down the blinds and we also gave them a 'door knock'. Now the door knock was crêpe, folded in, with a wee bit of tape to tie it to the knocker, and it had a bow on it. If a person was single it was a white bow; if they were married it was black. Generally in the country in the old days, you supplied the minister with a shoulder

David, aged twenty, with his parents before joining the family undertaking business 'Houston & Williamson'.

scarf that went over the shoulder and made a sash. Whenever they were arranging a funeral they would have said they wanted a 'shoulder scarf for the reverend so and so'.

The custom was to sit with the corpse. Now some may have sat all evening but after it came to about twelve, usually everybody went home to bed. But where it was a wake it was a different thing; they sat up all night for the wake. Generally there would be a case of stout, or Guinness as they call it, and maybe some whiskey, something like that. Of course, they all would get fairly happy and some even got hymn books out and sang a hymn or two. That was in the Protestant end, and of course in the Catholic end they did the same, they had their wakes too. Sometimes you could say it was more like a drunken spree. My experience was the Protestant could drink, but the Roman Catholic could show him how to drink, if you understand what I mean!

I heard tell that some of the boys would be up to their tricks. If the feet was facing the window, what did the boys do? They slipped in and tied strings to the body's hands and when it was at the height of the wake these boys crept up to the window, pulled the strings and of course the body sat up in the coffin. The people fled and they swore that the body had sat up in the coffin!

Most of the people in Belfast, especially the north of Belfast, were country people and no matter where they were they were sort of superstitious. Though some said they didn't believe in it, they wouldn't run any risk so they applied it just the same. If they had a mirror in the room they'd put a sheet over it – something to do with bad luck. And they had an impression that if they put a saucer with salt on it, it would keep the body from swelling. Of course it was neither doing it any good or harm, so when we were taking the coffin, we took the saucer off and sat it to one side. And whenever they saw a body with the mouth lying open, they thought it was the sign that there was going to be another death.

Generally people had one great fear, and that was to be buried a pauper. What a 'pauper' meant, the town buried them and buried them in the 'public', as we would call it. In England they would have called it the common grave. The people called it the 'pauper's grave'. It was a common grave that was opened and they buried one on top of the other, no matter who they were. They had a general record in the cemetery office, but as far as you were concerned they didn't know where they were buried. There must have been a good deal of it, because if you go into the city cemetery you will see large plots of land with no burial in them except round the edges. In other words, they sold the graves round the edge of the plot but in the centre was the public graves or common graves. If they died in the poorhouse and there was none belonging to them and none claimed the responsibility, it lay on the city to see the person buried and they were buried in the public ground.

As a matter of fact, no women went to the Protestant funerals in my early days, for years. Protestants were very particular. If there was a death in the street, the husband had to attend. It was disrespectful if he didn't turn up, and he always wore his good clothes, a black suit and a bowler hat. So if you had seen a Protestant funeral coming down the Crumlin Road, all you saw was hats, unless there was some children with bare heads. If you saw a Catholic funeral coming down, a lot of them had caps on. It wasn't that they had any less respect for the person, but those were the different customs.

I myself want to live as long as I can, but when the day comes, I'll feel my day is finished and I have no fear of it. But I'm not what they say, looking forward, saying, 'I can't wait to get away.' I'm still, in a way, clinging to this world, and I think everybody does.

David Williamson married and had four children. His eldest son, Archie, followed in his father's footsteps and they worked together until David's retirement at the age of eighty-seven. Archie says that had his father not lost his diving licence, he would have still been working to this day! Archie himself has now retired and his own sons have not been tempted to join the family firm, so Houston & Williamson has been sold, after three generations of Williamsons working there. David now lives happily in Bangor, Northern Ireland, with his daughter and son-in-law.

NORMAN COLLINS *was born in Hartlepool in 1897, the second son of well-educated parents. His father was a locomotive builder and a Methodist lay preacher. As a child, he was an avid reader, especially of boy's adventure stories of the sea or the jungle. He made his own first camera and loved to explore the local woodland, observing the wildlife there. When Norman volunteered for the Seaforth Highlanders, inspired by the glamour of the regiment, he little expected that one of his duties would be to bury in mass graves thousands of rotting bodies that had lain for months in no man's land on the battlefields of the Somme.*

When I was a boy, and very young too, I did dream of being a soldier, because my earliest memory was of the South African War and the Relief of Mafeking. In fact, only within recent years I have wondered why I ever brought myself not only to join the army but to join an infantry regiment. I actually joined up the day after the war was declared in 1914, August the 4th. A recruiting station opened near us and I went down there and told them I was twenty-one. I was seventeen. I went back home

and told my father. He was horrified. He said that I couldn't because I was only seventeen, and nineteen was the age for Kitchener's army. So when I was eighteen, I thought there is only one way to do it, which was to go and join up somewhere else. I got a ticket from the recruiting office in Stockton on Tees to Dingwall, north of Inverness. I said I'd go up there and join the Seaforth Highlanders. I got my ticket and with ten shillings in my pocket, I set off on Saturday morning, so I wasn't missed too much.

I was commissioned in August 1916 and went to France the following month. The battalions were due to go into action on the Somme. On July 1st of the same year, the Newfoundland regiment, amongst many, many others, dug in along the line of the Somme, and had attacked the village of Beaumont-Hamel, which was in effect a fortress. The Germans, who had machine-guns, practically decimated the Newfoundland regiment, and the bodies had rotted there after four and a half months. We had not moved our front line from that date, July 1st, until November 13th, when we attacked.

I was appointed burial officer, as I was the one detailed for the job. I was told to do the job and got on and did it. Of course, I had quite large squads of men to help me with picks and shovels, mainly shovels, and also stretchers. One thing I did feel was wrong, that they shouldn't have put the same men to collect the dead as had fought in the battle, because in many cases the men they picked up were their brothers and cousins. In a Highland regiment you would have a lot of people who joined up from the same village and from the same family. So I had the task with my burial parties of at least giving them some sort of burial.

I found that in almost every case the rats had made a nest in the cage of the chest and they ran out as we moved

Norman in the uniform of the Seaforth Highlanders in 1915.

them. This, I think, was one of my most horrible memories. They were well fed, the rats on the Somme. Big fat rats, almost as big as cats. We shovelled the rotting bodies into shell holes, which were very often filled with water, and probably put about twenty-five bodies in each. In the setting sun I remember the green and blue tinge to the water which looked rather beautiful. I think that had come from the copper of the shells. You see, each unexploded shell has a copper band round it, and there were many unexploded shells lying about which had to be avoided.

The hair in many cases continued to grow, but there was very little flesh on the face – it was more a skull. I remember distinctly that the putties they wore were still perfectly round until one stepped on them, and then they went flat because there was only the bone left.

But strangely enough, when bodies have lain out for some time, it doesn't become so repulsive. It is a sweet smell and I suppose one becomes used to it. They were all volunteers, they were all young men, and one thought, 'There but for the grace of God go I.' But it was not a job that I would recommend, especially for a young officer aged nineteen. And it didn't make me any braver when I had to go into another attack.

The pay books were in reasonably good condition, as I think they were contained in a sort of oil cloth which protected them. Photographs of mothers and fathers and their sweethearts and wives and children were all in the pay books, and of course their last will and testament, which I think didn't even need a witness. Oh, I don't know how many we collected, but it was a matter of hundreds. Hundreds of books which we carried back to brigade headquarters. And I noticed as we went that the communication trenches had bodies, parts of bodies, sticking out of the wall for quite a long way. The trench, I suppose, had been dug through the bodies where they lay. Occasionally you would see a loose head or two kicking about but apart from that, I suppose one got used to it.

The contrast, I remember, was going into a great dugout at brigade headquarters. Steps went down and at the bottom there were parcels from Fortnum and Mason's on the table, and it was another world. I remember being regaled to tea and cakes, having handed over my sandbags full of pay books, and I felt rather glad to get back to my own men. It was another world and I rather resented it. But there it is.

The parents of the soldiers who were killed, they were all written to by an officer who served in the same battalion, and very possibly in the same company. So they actually knew the man, you see. After the show, we used to sit down and we were given so many names and addresses and we had to compose a letter of condolence. Well of course, when you did so many, it tended to become a little stereotyped. But you tried, if possible, to put a little personal touch. I don't think we ever replied to the replies, otherwise we would have been entering into correspondence with scores of people we didn't know. I think it was an order that having done the letter, that was the end of it.

Also, after a show we had to leave a certain amount of wounded out in 'no man's land', we couldn't get them back. You could hear them during the following nights crying from pain and it affected us very much. We did try to go out at night and bring them back again, although with many of them you couldn't do anything for them, they were so badly wounded. I saw cases that obviously were going to die, and it was far better if you give them a dose of morphine, because we carried morphine sewn into our tunics. They just died, very often talking about their mother and their boyhood, that sort of thing. We were told how to put a bullet through the back of the head with a .45 revolver, which is completely painless I believe. I know it did happen but I did not do it, ever. You see, some of the wounds were terrible. When they had half their crotch blown away with a fragment of shell or their intestines were lying there and they knew they were dying, they would much rather, I'm sure, have been relieved of their misery. But it doesn't bear to think about it, it doesn't really.

One always had dreams. I did have one peculiar dream which occurred more than once. I dreamt that I was in the trench and I couldn't put my head up because I knew I was in France. Walking past me at eye-level were hundreds and thousands of boots, marching past. They went on and on and on, and I realised it was the dead all walking away and leaving me behind. I felt worried that I had been left behind, that I was still there. That was a very vivid dream for a long, long time.

Over a million British were killed and I think altogether, including the Germans, the French and Russians, it might have been twenty-five million. It was a whole generation destroyed. The people who were born between 1890, who would have been twenty-four when the war broke out, and 1900, that generation, they were practically all wiped out.

The years of the war seemed to last longer than all of the rest of my life put together. I remember looking at my father and thinking he had never seen a dead man and I'd seen scores and scores of dead men. He had never seen a man shot, never seen a man die, or if he had it would have been in pleasant family circumstances, with no pain attached to it maybe. So I really felt much older than my parents and I think that feeling continued for the rest of my life.

Following the Armistice, Norman Collins went out to serve with the Indian Army on the North-West Frontier. In 1921 he was wounded and sent back home. He then went to Durham University and on graduation took up an apprenticeship with the Austin Motor Company. Norman continued working in the transport industry, often travelling extensively throughout the world, until he retired in 1961.

In 1987 he returned to the French battlefields of the First World War and was awarded the Somme Medal for his service in the field. Married, with two children, he occasionally shoots, and with his tractor he works his remarkable garden, with five thousand roses, and fruit trees, and oaks from acorns which were brought from Arnhem.

•

KATHLEEN DAYUS *was a child of the inner city, born in 1903 among the workshops of Birmingham's 'jewellery quarter', where her father was a caster. She was the last of thirteen children. 'I was the youngest, yes that's what they call it, the baker's dozen. I was scraping the pot.' Only seven survived to adulthood. Kathleen's mother ruled them with a fierce temper and a quick hand, from which her gentler father was unable to protect them. She grew up in poverty, with cramped living conditions and inadequate food. But Kathleen loved school and read whatever she could — even if it was scraps of newspaper covering the table. She turned for love and affection to her eldest sister, Mary, and to her granny.*

Me dad says, 'You'd better take granny some coal in the little cart.' It was used for everything that cart, so I put the two lumps of coal in there. Mum says, 'Only take one,' but I took two and of course dad covered it over with a sack and I took it to grandma's. Well it was icy-cold day and there was freezing snow on the ground. My mum used to say to me, if we went of an errand, she used to say, 'Now get your clean drawers on in case you get knocked down with the horses,' because there was a lot

of horses in them days. Well, I wondered why she used to say that but in later years I realised that she didn't want the neighbours to know I'd got dirty underclothes on if I met with an accident. But anyway, this day, she didn't change me clean drawers.

I took the cart to me granny's with the coal in, and I were running along when all of a sudden I heard some horses at the back. I looked round and there was two of 'em and they was coming towards me. I was terrified of those horses, so as I run along, I slipped and landed inside this wet fish shop. There was sawdust all wet and icy and as I slipped, I grabbed hold of a slab of sprats and herrings and pulled 'em down on top of me; ice, and fish, all over me, on the floor. There I lay and I'm crying. In came the man from the back and he says, 'What's going on here?' So I said, 'Oh, I've slipped down and I'm frightened of horses and I ain't got me clean drawers on.' And I can remember, I can see him now, starting to laugh. He said, 'Well, of all the things I've heard,' he said, 'I've never heard that.' And he lifted me up and he took me outside and I went on to me granny's.

When I got to me granny's there was all the neighbours on the step outside, and they were crying. I couldn't understand this, so I said, 'Can I open the door, Mrs Phipps?' – that was one of the neighbours, Mrs Phipps. I said, 'I want to give me granny this coal.' So Mrs Phipps says, 'Oh, 'er wouldn't have need of it where 'er's going' – 'cos they were very rough, people in them days. Anyway, I took the coal and said, 'Well, where's my granny?' They said, 'Her's dead, her's had her chips.'

I didn't stop any longer. I run all the way home with me cart and when I got in the house mum said, 'Now, what's the matter with you?' I said, 'Me granny's dead. She's had 'er chips.' She said, 'What're you talking about.' So I said, 'Her's dead, her's dead – Mrs Phipps told me 'er's dead.' So her says, 'Well, where's the coal?' So I said, 'Well, Mrs Phipps had it.' She says, 'Come on,' she says, 'I'll show her.' So on went her cap, this was the sort that mum was – on went dad's cap, off went her apron, and down the street she marched – she never walked, she always used to march. She wasn't afraid of anybody. Down the street she went. 'Come on,' she says, 'bring the cart.' So I'm taking the cart, following behind, looking to see if there was any more horses.

We gets to me granny's, and mum demands her coal from Mrs Phipps, who only brought out one lump, put it in the cart. We went in the house and all I could see was granny's rocking chair. As mum shut the door, the rocking chair started to move and all I could see was granny's bits of paper sticking out of her 'ead, as curlers in her hair. I was frightened to death, because I'd never seen a dead person before. So I looked at her, and I looked a bit more, and I put me hand over me eyes like that, and I peeked through and I says, 'Granny's got her eyes open and 'er's looking at you.' 'Don't be daft,' she said. So I said, ''Er are, look, 'er's looking at you.' So she said, 'I'll soon settle that,' and she shuts Granny's eyes and leaves her in the rocking chair there.

Then she said, 'You've got to stop with your gran while I go and fetch the neighbours in to help me lay her out.' And she locked me in. I couldn't believe that she'd do such a thing. I was so scared, I wet me drawers with fright. I still kept looking at granny, her eyes were open again and she was staring straight at the fireplace.

Well, she fetched the two neighbours and they go and carry her upstairs and wash her and lay her out. Mum tells 'em they can come to the funeral and thanks 'em very much for their help. While they've gone, I sat by the side of the bed and I'm still looking at gran. Well, the pennies must have come off, her eyes were still open and I said, 'Mum, grandma's still awake, look. Er's looking at you.' Mum said, 'Oh don't be barmy.' Anyway, she closes the eyes again and puts on two more pennies. But all the while I sat there, mum opened all the drawers and took all her few coppers, half crowns and a tin of farthings, and put them all in her pocket, underneath her apron. Me dad and me brother, I think, went to fetch the undertaker.

Course when they're laid out, they're laid out in the bed upstairs, then the undertaker brings the coffin to the house. It isn't like that today – they put 'em in these 'beauty parlours'; what they call 'em? Anyway, in those days they bring the coffin to the house and they put 'em in the coffin and put it on the table under the window, or wherever there was room, 'cos there was only little rooms we lived in. And then all the neighbours used to come round and look at 'em.

But she was a lovely old gran, I always loved her. When she died I broke me heart. When she lay in her coffin on the table in the front room, I put a little note in her hand to take to heaven with her. I was only young and when I felt her hand, it was stiff and cold. I went ever so queer. I can still feel that hand as I talk about it, do you know that? Now, today, I can still feel those still cold fingers.

So the blinds had to be drawn, all through the waiting days – sometimes a fortnight – before they buried them. We had paper blinds and those was pulled down and we had to have that day and night, the blinds drawn. When the funeral went past the street, the shopkeepers and all the neighbours would come out and you'd see 'em raise their hats. The traffic'd stop as if they were royalty. Very good in those days.

The undertakers always wore a black top hat, frock-tailed coat, black gloves and a white handkerchief with a black border round. We had white handkerchiefs and white gloves, but they always had black. There was black ribbon on the horses; lovely, lovely horses. I was never scared of them horses 'cos they looked so well groomed and their coats so shiny.

Kate's formidable mother in 1932. Behind are Kate's sister Mary (right) and Mary's daughter whose baby is on Kate's mother's lap.

But the corporation horses and the dustman's cart – I used to be scared of them 'cos they was them shire horses.

Everybody got together at funerals: there was aunts, uncles, cousins, and people they thought was cousins or relatives – but they had to walk. Sometimes if they was better off, they'd have another extra coach to put 'em in, but most of 'em followed behind 'cos they went very slow then.

Well, mother had the insurance money and she spent it on herself. She bought some new shoes, button-up boots and new hat and coat. I always remember that hat, a big black hat with a big black bird on top. She used to preen herself, you know, think it was wonderful, 'cos she never liked granny anyway. Mary my sister said, 'You've spent all that insurance money on yourself. What about the kids?' So mum said, 'Oh, I'll see to that when I've bought the other things for the funeral.' And Mary said,

'Well, I'm buying some clothes for Katy and Frankie and Liza out of my wages this week.' So she bought me a white frock and some white shoes and a black sash, and I kept that black sash for me hair, because I only had little plaits and I used to have string on the end of 'em. Then after the funeral Mary locked 'em in a trunk, so mum couldn't pawn them.

Anyway, at the church mum was preening herself. She wanted to let the neighbours see what she was dressed like, you know? So one of the neighbours says, 'Who do you think 'er is, the Queen of Sheba?' And there was a 'shhhh' that went round the church. Dad says, 'Move up the aisle.' He says, 'You're stopping all the congregation. You're making a spectacle of yourself.' But you'd think there was a train coming through the place the way they all went 'shhh'.

Then there was all the neighbours and everybody round the graveside and the parson was saying 'Ashes to ashes, dust to dust ...,' and little Jonesy piped, 'And if God don't have you, the devil must.' His father hit him and he fell down the next hole, he did, and of course his wife started to cry. His dad said, 'I'll give him "the devil must" when I get home.' And the parson looked up and said, 'The Lord forgive them for they know not what they do'!

After grandma was buried, all the neighbours that had helped to lay her out, the six bearers and me dad and mum and the family all sat down to table. And Frankie, me brother, he'd got a cold, he didn't go to the funeral and he was sitting by the fire. Our black cat, Peat, always used to be under the table when anybody was eating, waiting for bits and scraps that was thrown down to him. All of a sudden dad says, 'Where's the cat? Where's our Peat?' Frankie says, 'Oh dad, he went out in the rain and I put him in the oven to dry.' We'd got a roaring fire, so dad flashed to the oven and opened the oven door and there's the cat, its hair all up, and it went straight out through the window. Frankie had a walloping off mum, up the stairs he had to go, so he didn't have any of the feast.

The feast was nothing elaborate. They'd have corned meat, pigs pudding, cheese and pickles, and a gallon of ale on the table – always had to have a gallon of ale. Everybody had a drink before the funeral and after the funeral. And after everything was done, they'd go up to the George and Dragon, and get drunk, and they'd talk about one another and the old times.

Kathleen was married in 1921 when she was two months' pregnant, and went to live in the attic of her mother's house. Altogether she had five children. But she lost her first, and her last was born two days after her husband died.

When my little boy was six he had the measles and I kept him at home. After the six weeks, the school board man came and said they'd summons me if I didn't send him to school. So he went back. Well, three days after, I had news to say that he had been knocked down by the butcher's van, on the Sandpits, that was just below the school.

His dad had given him a pig's bladder as a football and they used to blow that up to play with it in the yard. Well, mum says, 'I ain't having that bloody thing in here,' she said – oh she was a darling – 'it stinks, take it out.' So anyway, his dad and me little son used to hide it down the cellar. One day when me little son went to pick it up, it wasn't there – it was all bits and pieces. The rats had chewed it. Dad brought another one, and he hid it outside the attic window where we was living.

So when my boy was killed, I used to look at that bladder and I used to cry. I wouldn't let me other children go outside because I was frightened they'd come to the same fate. So anyway, when I looked at this bladder, I kept crying, and my husband said he was going to get rid of it. 'Oh no you're not,' I said. 'It stays there.' One day I looked up and it was missing, it had gone. So he said, 'I've buried it by the side of his little grave.' And I went down there and he'd made a big hole by the side and he'd buried the bladder. I still looked at the bare wall and watched for a long while, but gradually it got better, 'cos, you know, I'd got the other children to pacify me mind, to make me forget a little bit.

Kathleen Dayus was left a widow after seven years' marriage. Her father died in a workhouse, where her mother had had him placed after he had a stroke. Her mother and sister were killed in a raid during the Second World War. She was forced through economic necessity to leave her children in a Dr Barnardo's home, and only after a great struggle was she allowed to have them home again eight years later. She now has twelve grandchildren and as many great-grandchildren.

At the age of seventy-two, Kathleen started writing. It took her five years, writing 'a little bit each night', until her first book Her People *was finished. Virago Press have now published four volumes of her autobiography and Birmingham University have recently given her an honorary Master of Arts degree.*

Writing has given Kathleen a new lease of life: 'Now I love to go out, meet people me own age. I go on trips, I been to America to see me youngest daughter who lives in Florida. Stayed a month and we had a fortnight in Disneyland.' And at the age of ninety-two she heard that her life story is to be made into a film.

Writing my books, I think that's made me live longer. I'm living again, I've got something to live for. And I think how lucky I am to be fit and healthy. I think people died younger in those days; it was through hard work and worry and the trials and tribulations they had. Can you imagine – no work and no food and struggling? It was certainly survival of the fittest in those days. I never think about death, death at all for myself. I think, 'Well, when I go, I've lived me life, I've suffered, but I've enjoyed life.'

7 And They Sailed Away

The seven children of the Summerhayes family were born in the small hillside village of Amberley in the Cotswolds. Their father, Henry Summerhayes, had become the vicar of Amberley church in 1892 and shortly afterwards his wife Emily gave birth to their first daughter, Mercy. Over the next thirteen years, four more daughters and two sons were born – Grace, Christopher, Eirene, Mary, Noel and Julius.

The family lived in a large rambling vicarage next to the church, looked after by four maids, a nanny for the children and a governess who came on her bicycle every day to teach them – they did not attend the local village school. From an early age they learnt from their parents' example of how to serve others, whether by visiting the sick of the parish or by collecting money for their individual missionary boxes. And even as children, as Mary recalls, they dreamt of a future when they would be working in Africa, still sustained by their parents' efforts: 'We'll be missionaries. And Mummy and Daddy'll sit home and thread beads, to send out to Africa.'

They were a close-knit family who as children relied on one another for companionship. And across the lane lived their granny.

The Summerhayes family having tea in their grandmother's house in Gloucestershire. From left to right: Julius, Mary, Noel, Mercy, Eirene and Grace.

By 1914 Henry Summerhayes had become headmaster of St Michael's, a school for the children of missionaries in Surrey. From left to right: Mercy, Grace, mother, Christopher, father, Eirene, Mary. In front: Julius and Noel.

EIRENE I always remember in church she used to wear a sealskin cape, and I would rub my face against it, you know, in church, a lovely feeling! Granny was always there; she was like a second mother. We used to go over to lunch on Saturdays always, and she would come to lunch with us on Sundays, always with sixpence for our missionary box. It must have cost her quite a lot – she used to always put something in and we all had a missionary box.

Four of us slept together in one room. We lived in the nursery on the first floor and we looked out over a lovely view, across the hills – I grew up with those views and it was nice really, the Rectory. We only went downstairs to say goodnight. They were having supper; we used to go in and say goodnight, then we used to have to walk from the dining room through the drawing room in the dark, we had to shut the doors and it was very bogey – we used to hurry through it. We only went to Sunday lunch, we didn't have any meals otherwise in the dining room; we were in the nursery.

We had a nanny, a wonderful nanny – she really was – but she was very stern and she had a very hurtful hand. But you know, we all loved her.

GRACE We had such a firm disciplinarian nurse and we weren't allowed to cry, because if we cried she'd say, 'Put out your hand Miss Gracie and I'll give you something to cry for.' So you learnt very early on not to cry, which was a good idea.

MARY We were very happy. I don't remember quarrelling. We didn't have a lot of friends. We were sufficient to ourselves, I think.

GRACE Mercy was the boss and Christopher and I used to gang up against her and do dreadful things. We knew she didn't like cows so we chased the cows all the way down the stony path in the churchyard into the Rectory garden until she fell and cut herself quite badly. Christopher was sent to bed and I was not. I always thought that was very good politics; if they sent us both to bed we should have been ganging up together again but Christopher was sent to bed and I was left miserably to wander round the garden.

MERCY Well, if you are the eldest, you are always told to see that the others are good. When we went to parties my mother would say, 'Now be sure that they're all good children, won't you?' So I got a lot of anxiety grey hairs from that.

GRACE What immediately comes to my mind is father with a cricket bat, not father in the pulpit. He was a very good preacher too, and a very good sportsman. I can even see the look on his face, how he set his lips when he did a special stroke with his bat. So he led the lads of the village in football and cricket as well as in worship. He was quite fierce with us. I remember being sent to bed and that sort of thing, which I always used to think was grossly unfair.

In those days there was a lot of drunkenness in the village, really drunk old men. They used to go to the village pub, the Amberley Inn probably. One night, quite late, in the dark, there was a knock on the door and father went to it. 'You'll be surprised to see me Rector. I be a-come to sign the pledge.' So father in an expansive mood said, 'Oh well old Joe, if you do, I will too.' So father there and then signed the pledge and instead of being able to drink his glass of claret with Granny Whitemore every week, it had to be old toast water. Do you know what toast water is? It's just hot water poured on toast and that's supposed to be a good drink to make up for alcohol.

I remember that I used to go with him every Monday morning to open the school. I used to toddle along with him and think this was great fun. But my mother and father were very busy because mother seemed to be the mother of the whole village and would even sit up with families with whooping cough and things like that. But she had her fleet of maids to look after the Rectory in those days. It was a very cumbersome sort of Rectory, rather elegant to look at, but it's been pulled down now and instead there's a stupid little utilitarian one.

EIRENE My mother was a wonderful person: she never had any favourites, she loved us all, and she used to make you feel you were very important. She used to say, 'Oh Eirene May, mother's own pet,' and, you know, she was a very lovable person. She used to play the piano, she was very musical, and taught us all to sing. We used to stand in a row in the drawing room and give concerts. People used to come.

I used to go for walks with mother and she used to take me around to see the old ladies of the village, which I enjoyed really, though they were poor old things. Poor old Mrs Winterbottom, she was bedridden, mother used to go and see if she was all right. Then there was another old lady who lived up by Mr Griffins, who was also bedridden, and she used to have mice in her bed! I remember I was horrified, but she did! I saw them; they just passed through ...

I can remember mother bringing back a baby once in a drawer, 'cos there was a woman in the village who had got a huge family and then she had another. Mother thought she couldn't manage to look after it. She brought it back. It stayed with us and our nanny for a little while. They were a very hardworking pair.

Christopher and I, when we were children, used to be 'Mr and Mrs Jones,' and we used to hold tea parties. We had a little table in the window of the nursery and we had a doll's tea-set, a little teapot and things, and pretended – we used to make polite conversation: 'Did your cook make this cake?' And so on. When he went to school, I hobnobbed with Mary and Grace, you know one younger, one older. Anyway, we managed. We were all very fond of each other and when we used to go out, we always stuck together. People used to say when we went to parties, 'Oh, the Summerhayes family, they stick together.' Still, we did.

MARY At family meals, once a week one or other of us had to produce a FACT, an instructive fact. The only one I can remember was, 'It's never dry weather when seagulls are on land.' That was because they used to come up on the Common, the seagulls. Yes, I remember mother saying, 'Oh go and look in the dictionary dear if you don't know what that means.' Quite a lot of education went on round meal times.

MERCY Whit Monday was a wonderful day. We had a band in church, a large brass band, and then we went out of the church and had a big tea, and then after the tea we marched along with the band all the way to a field where we had races for children. We enjoyed Whit Monday like anything. It was a wonderful day.

An old colonel who lived at Sheepscombe used to make lantern slides, and we used to go for tea and be shown some. One was 'Little Black Sambo' – which he made all by himself from the pictures in the little book. He painted them on slides and we used to sit enthralled while he showed us these pictures of Little Black Sambo. Nowadays, people say that's racist, but it was a very thrilling story for us.

In 1908 their father left Amberley to take a living in Hampstead, London, but he was essentially a 'country parson' and after six years he accepted a headship at St Michael's at Limpsfield in Surrey, a church missionary school, where he remained until 1928. It was during this period that his 'young birds flew the nest'.

Mercy, born in 1892, was the first to leave. At the age of twenty-five she set out for Alert Bay on Canada's west coast.

MERCY I was asked to go to Canada because the man who used to teach Indian boys in a school on the west coast of British Columbia was called up in the war. They didn't know what to do for a teacher so they asked me if I'd come and teach about thirty great big Indian boys.

It was quite a long journey in those days and the war was still on. It was very rough on the Atlantic and all mothers with babies were seasick. I was a very good sailor, I loved the sea and I didn't mind how rough it was, so I used to go round and collect all the babies and look after them. Then when we got to Canada, we had a long journey all across Canada until we got to the Rocky Mountains; then a wonderful train journey through those magnificent mountains to Vancouver and at Vancouver we got on a little steamer to go up to where this school was in Alert Bay.

In those days, Indians were given an allowance to live on their own island but the allowance said that they couldn't have any strong drink. So it was peaceful, in a sense. The boys used to go to their homes for the holidays. But then I went back about thirty years later everything had changed. The government had now allowed them to have drink, and half of the Indians were drunk and the school wasn't at all the same. It was very sad, and it upset me very much really.

The great wealth of the Indians was the cedar trees. They used the bark to make their clothes and they cut these great tall trees down to make totem poles. They built their houses of great cedar logs and four or five Indian families would live in one communal house with a chief. The chief had his totem pole outside and they earned their living by fishing for salmon. There was also a cannery on the island where the fish were put into tins. So they were very, very rich in cedar trees and salmon.

I was teaching them very simple ABC – because they had to be taught in English. Each tribe, each village, had its own – well – language really. The Indians used to go to church and have English services. It seemed rather sad, but it couldn't be helped because although their basic

A portrait of Mercy taken in Canada where she taught native Indians in 1917.

language was called Kwa Kwala they had all kinds of different versions of it.

When they knew that the salmon season was coming they went out in their long canoes across to where the mouth of the river was and they sat silently waiting for the salmon to come. Nobody knew exactly when they would come, but they knew the time of year and they sat there very patiently. It was wonderful, the silence by that river; all those canoes sitting and waiting. And then suddenly one salmon jumped out of the river and that showed them that there was a school of salmon coming. So then, no more silence; they all leapt into their canoes and paddled hard, dropping a net behind them enclosing this big school of fish. Then they had to pull all the net in and it went on and on and on, and you thought, 'Oh they haven't got anything this time,' but at the end there was a great gleaming mass of salmon. And they took these salmon over to the cannery and the women put them in tins – then into the ovens. If you wanted a fish, you'd say to one of the boys in the school, 'Oh run down to the cannery, ask them to give us a fish.' And they'd come back with an enormous fish, nothing to pay because there was such a wealth of salmon. I think now the Japanese go with great big motor ships and that the fishing isn't the same.

The Indians didn't go in for cooking the fish very much. They dried it, hung up, so smoked salmon comes from the Indians. Then they loved a dish of fish oil. It was very, very rich in vitamins, but it had a most terrible smell. If you got any of it on your clothes, you had to go and have a new suit, the smell was so bad. But to the Indians this ulucan oil meant everything. When we had that dreadful flu later on, this fish oil really saved a good many Indian lives, because it was so full of vitamins.

That flu epidemic came all over the world at once. It was dreadful in England, it was dreadful all across Canada, and it came to the Indian villages. All the boys lay there, very, very ill. There were some men in the wireless station, and they came and helped us. I was lying on the floor. I couldn't do anything, I was so ill. They said, 'What have we got to do with the boys?' And I said, 'Cook them some stew, make them something.' And they said, 'Well how do we do that?!' They really saved the boys' lives, and mine too.

When the war was over I left Alert Bay and some Canadian friends said, 'Why don't you come to our university, because you've nearly got your degree in London and you'd only have to do one more year.' So I went to the University of Edmonton in Canada, a wild woolly-west university. Then for a little while I taught in the Canadian prairie schools, one-room schools where all the children gathered. They came to school on horseback most of them, or little rigs, and they were so pleased to come, I taught them all I could. The whole room was lined with blackboards, so I could have somebody doing geography, and somebody doing maths in another corner, somebody else doing something else somewhere else.

I used to ride to school every day, and we'd put all our horses loose in the field. When it was time to go home, I'd say, 'Now children you've got to go slow today in your little rigs. Don't let me hear you galloping away like you do generally' – 'Yeah teacher.' So off they set and I stood by the school door, but as soon as they were out of sight they galloped for anything, for of course they were so used to riding horseback.

I too used to go for long forty-mile rides, that kind of thing, and I enjoyed the rough riding. But in Canada, they have these great big saddles, so there's always something to hold on to. You're quite safe, you hold on, you don't get thrown off. Though I did get chucked off sometimes.

Out in Canada Mercy felt a sense of freedom: 'in a way – the world was before you'. On her return she continued teaching, eventually ending up a social worker and working as a Children's Officer for Reading. She now lives in her own house in Painswick, Gloucestershire, near to her sister Grace. They meet for tea on a regular basis.

Grace, the second child, was born in 1895. She was going to study at Cambridge but was unable to do so because of the First World War. Instead:

GRACE I went to Northumberland and taught for four blessed years. I taught everything: Latin, maths, history, hockey, singing, everything. Looking back on it I think they used me quite a lot. I enjoyed it, but I was very glad when the war rescued me! I already belonged to the Red Cross and I got into a British military hospital in Herne Bay. But I thought I'd never get to France that way and – I had a friend – so I joined up with the Scottish Women's Hospital detachment. And I went to France, yes: steaming across the Channel with two warships guarding the passenger road.

I went to this big old abbey which was mysterious and cold. But the first night I had to help carry a little slim French girl – dead. And what was she doing in a military hospital? Well, we had a very good woman surgeon, and the village had no one and she was brought in in extreme labour. She died there and I had to help carry her, poor little lady. But she was my first patient.

We kept the bedpans in the pulpit, we had the refectory as the ward; I suppose we had about twenty beds each side. Very often people were shovelled in the beds before you had time to change the blood-soaked sheets from the last patient, at moments when the fighting was severe. Then I got put into an officers' ward, which I didn't like at all. They weren't acutely ill, they were convalescent, and there was a terrible Sister who used to say, 'Summerhayes! Take the men out for a walk.' And I used to have to take them to the village for an amble, and beg them for my sake not to go into the pub. But I thought that didn't seem to be what I'd come out to France for.

We had mostly French, some Americans. We knew that things were getting awfully muddled up at the front when we got a mixture of people coming in. We got some Algerians, poor men. They'd been lugged over, I suppose, from Algeria or somewhere to serve in the French army. One took it for granted that men were bloody minded and would fight, and it was our business as nurses to go and help them. But I sometimes

A studio portrait of Grace taken before she went to teach in Northumberland.

And They Sailed Away 177

think now that I wouldn't go again; they can get on with it without our mending them up again, but I don't know if that would be at all moral!

We had a camp hospital up near the front where we were quite close to the action and heard the, you know, roar of it all. What I was afraid of there was not the bombs dropping – the bombs used to sort of drop in the distance and make an awful noise – that didn't wake me, but the rats did and at the scratch of a rat I would wake up and fling my shoes over the hut. I was very afraid of the rats.

My friend and I had gone out with our bicycles – I don't think you would be allowed to do that now. So we bicycled to Chartres and Beauvais and all those lovely places. We bicycled to Paris once for the weekend and Paris was so lovely. That was my first view of Paris. It was springtime, and frost – and as there were no cars because of the war – I remember now how beautiful it was.

After the war Grace returned to England and qualified as a doctor at the Royal Free Hospital in London. She worked for four years as a doctor in England before:

The Student Christian Movement asked me to apply for a job in East Africa. When I went they said, 'Oh that one's gone but they do need a doctor to start up a maternity hospital in Ghana – the Gold Coast.' So I was interviewed by a large group of men round a table, no women, who told me all about this new hospital they were going to open and how difficult it would be and all the rest of it. Then one of them said, 'And do you think you could do this?' I realised that this was one of the moments when you pull yourself together and sell yourself. So I said, 'Yes, I think I should do it perfectly', and I was appointed. I think you have to be humble up to a certain point, don't you, and then at the right moment you have to really sell yourself.

The journey out was so terrible, I thought, 'Oh how awful; now I shall have to stay here for the rest of my life because I shall never dare to come back again.' Of course I did, about ten times. I had to get used to it because obviously we didn't fly then. Makes all the difference flying now, but a long fortnight's voyage is no fun being awfully seasick.

When I got there, there was a nice empty hospital. We got it properly furnished and equipped and everything, then Sister and I sat in the hospital waiting for some patients. We wondered whether we would ever get any because both the witch doctors and the people were against us. I think they didn't really want us. So I sent a summons to all the witch doctors to come and have tea with me at the hospital. The Africans like having tea parties and afterwards I got up onto the platform and addressed them. I said that I hadn't come to take away their patients, but if they got into any trouble they were welcome to bring me their messes. And then the next day we looked up and there was one of these old women bent double, with a row of eighteen little pregnant girls following behind her! We were in business! I did the first Caesarean birth out there, and this was a tremendous thing for them to see. The next day they all came saying, 'We want our babies the easy way', and I had to explain to them that it wasn't necessarily the easy way and I'm afraid I couldn't oblige!

At Christmas time we used to have a Christmas tree outside the hospital all lit up. It was very gay. My husband-to-be, who was a medical officer next door, went secretly down to the plantation with his big car and had a lovely tree cut down and brought to me. All the women who had had babies in the hospital during the year used to be invited and we had a great party round this tree. We used to sing Ghanaian songs and the women had lovely head-dresses on and looked very beautiful: all these women sitting round singing and laughing, because the Ghanaians do a lot of laughing – which is a good idea.

They're very friendly, and they were pleased with us for coming. My nurses were very charming people and I started a school of training, proper training. The officials wanted them to do an inferior kind of semi-training and I said, 'No. A baby is just the same whether it's African or English, and the nurses must be highly trained exactly the same as in London.' So we did just that.

Grace returned to England from Ghana at the beginning of the Second World War with her husband and two children, and worked as a GP in a village only a few miles away from her childhood home in Amberley. She looked after her mother until she died and is now herself a widow, living in her own house in Gloucestershire. She still sings in her local church.

Mary Stuart, born in 1900, had, according to her sisters, both beauty and brains. Eirene remembers that even as a baby Mary was admired: 'We used to go out for walks – "Oh! Isn't she lovely!" – and I used to toddle on beside the pram and – "Oh! Isn't she sweet!" Then when we went to school she was very bright and came out top of all England in her prelim exams.' Mary's younger sister Noel remembers her as 'not a good companion to me because she was always reading. She was a very bookie little girl. She'd put her fingers into her ears, like that, and say "Go away".'

Mary won a place at Cambridge, although at that time women students were not made welcome.

MARY When I was at Girton the whole university had voted against giving women degrees, so there was a certain amount of hostility in the air. Going into lectures the men used to stamp their feet and shout 'hoo! hoo!' and it taught you to keep your nose in the air. But I loved Cambridge. The autumn was beautiful there, October, the beginning of the Cambridge year. On market days I used to get big bunches of chrysanthemums for a shilling, put them in my bicycle basket and trundle out with them; chrysanthemums and golden trees. I learnt then to love the open skies which mother had always talked about from her Lincolnshire childhood.

Mary met her husband, Simon, when cycling and they were married as soon as she graduated. She wanted to work in India, having studied some Sanskrit at Cambridge, but instead she was sent with her husband, full of high expectations, to Accra, in the Gold Coast (later Ghana).

My expectations were thwarted. I thought I was going to help start the girls' school in Achimota, which was a new university started by the government, but I had a letter from the principal saying, 'We're looking forward to your housekeeping,' which was a shock, never having done any and not being interested in housekeeping at all. They had a staff of five men lodging in a big colonial house in Accra, waiting for the college to be built, and I was the first wife – the first woman to arrive. My poor husband with a new wife who hated what she was being told to do, which was to housekeep for these men, with a rather drunken African cook to help, I always remember. So my first impressions were disappointment. I found myself living in a semi-colonial town, Accra, with big European houses. One of my jobs was to take calling cards round in the car for the principal to the government officials' houses etc, which I loathed to do. So I wasn't very nice to know really. I wasn't enjoying it much.

It was in the days when they were working hard on research for yellow fever, which was the scourge of Africa then, the White Man's Grave. We were given injections of what they thought was the first yellow fever inoculations. I don't know why, but I was the only one who really succumbed to – it must have been yellow fever, or a very violent jaundice. I was in hospital there for quite a bit and I remember everybody used to bring in bunches of lavender-coloured orchids, tall orchids from the bush, and this tall lavender orchid is mixed in my mind with jaundice. I began to really hate that colour afterwards.

When we first were going out to Africa, I imagined ourselves on safari in the bush, à la Livingstone, and all that kind of thing. I had made for myself khaki-coloured short knickerbockers and a tunic, with leather boots, and these I thought were my safari outfit. Of course when you find

Above: 'Mary had both beauty and brains'. Top: With Julius who also went to Africa as a missionary doctor in Uganda.

yourself living in Accra that was not the kind of thing that you wore at all. However, when I was convalescing we were sent up country to the Cameroon hills and I thought, 'At last, I can put on my khaki suit.' Off we went in a lorry, which was the way one travelled in those days, and there was our host waiting for us at the bottom of the hills with this carrying chair and four porters. They had brought the chair to take me up the hill as it was rather steep. I was so furious. 'Oh dear!' my husband said, 'you must try to be gracious.' So I tried to be a little more gracious and I finally was carried up the hill, boots first, in this carrying chair. My first African safari! I don't think I ever wore those things again. I'd got an entirely romantic picture of African travel. But if you went out in colonial days to a colonial town, it was an utterly different life really.

I couldn't have pleased my parents more than marrying a man who turned out to be the Bishop of Uganda. Because Uganda was their great missionary theme. But his job officially was enormous: Uganda and quite a bit of Congo and down into Ruanda – now there are twenty bishops at least doing his job. Which was to get in our car, pack the lorry and have an African driver/cook with us – my husband always did the driving though – and off we'd go, perhaps twenty-five miles, to visit a village church and school We would probably camp in the village school, which might be mud and thatch or might be a bit bigger, and there'd be a confirmation service in the morning, and a very long communion service after that. In the afternoon, off to some little subsidiary village church more into the bush. Then probably the next morning, pack up and go another fifty miles – do the same sort of thing in another centre. On and on, and on. I think it's right to say about two-thirds of our life was travelling like that, on and around. It was all very friendly and we enjoyed it, and of course the further you go west, the more lovely it becomes. I remember saying to my husband. 'We're lucky to do this without paying for it aren't we?'

I went to church, sat through the long services with a faint air of patience, I hope. But on the whole I enjoyed it because Africans are just beautiful to contemplate. I used to love watching them moving up and down, the services. Then in the afternoon, perhaps I'd have a group of women to talk to; sometimes very long and hot, but I liked to be there because I found them all so very beautiful.

We went sometimes into the Congo forest, to little wee pygmy churches. My husband was a very big man and he'd stand up among these little pygmy people. It was priceless to see them gazing up into the skies singing very loudly. Then, off we'd go again, and more forest path, and another little church the next morning, which I enjoyed very much. I always longed to get to the walking part of the safaris, but it mostly was driving. When a former bishop came out and stayed with us once, we were going into the west, and he said, 'I used to do this on my bicycle.' I said, 'I know, we can't help having cars!' Well you had to of course, you couldn't possibly have got round without.

Among the pygmies was really going where they hadn't seen anybody like you before; it was sort of gaping interest – what we should say in England 'Oh my!' But that was only in the remoter parts. In Ruanda, the aristocratic tribe there were very tall men, and they liked my husband because he was the same sort of height so they could talk to him eye to eye. I think they liked to acknowledge the feeling that they were treated with equal respect when one met them.

On the far western border, on a little island in the middle of a beautiful lake – very remote – was a leper colony we used to go to. I always remember him confirming the lepers, just a few each time, with one of the white sisters following with an enamel basin of disinfectant. Before he went on to anybody else, he had to dip his hands into a disinfectant because leprosy was thought to be very infectious still. I don't mean he was in danger, but it was just a matter of cleanliness. Some of them were very, very crippled, and never would be better, but even then it could be arrested and a certain amount of painkilling was possible.

I was frightened once. I woke up and saw a black man pulling the blanket off my bed when I was sleeping on the veranda. I let out an enormous roar because my husband was sleeping inside. After a time nothing happened. I said, 'Did you hear me?' He said, 'Yes, I thought you were having a nightmare.' I was!

My husband took danger very calmly, because there were times towards the end of our stay, especially when there were nationalist movements going on, when he was meant to be shot. There was the time when he chose the first assistant bishop, African, from the west – a very fine man, everybody agreed, and it was high time, as he knew. But the nationalists of our local folk were very angry that he'd not chosen one of them and said if he went on with this appointment he was going to be shot. So we had soldiers sitting behind the bushes in our garden, waiting for this episode that might happen. I stayed at home just in case the corpse was carried back or whatever, but he took these dangerous moments with great calm, I must say.

In the end we felt we were educating the people to take a lead in government, or medicine or whatever. You didn't imagine that they were going to be underlings for ever, at all. In the beginning I didn't think about it a lot, because it was just beginning then, but it gathered speed as the years went on, which was just what people were after, of course, and what they deserved.

Mary and her husband had two sons and continued to live in Uganda until the country's independence. They retired to Cornwall, but then settled in a community for retired people in Surrey when Mary's husband became ill. She is now a widow. She enjoys travelling to visit her extensive family, continues to write, and composes special poems to commemorate family events.

Noel Marshall, the fifth Summerhayes daughter, born in 1902, had a great love of botany and music, and could have excelled in either field, but because funds were limited she was unable to go to university. Instead she trained to be a teacher, and 'discovered that's what I really wanted to do'. She taught for a time at St Michael's, her father's missionary school in Surrey, and then applied for a post in Nigeria to teach orphan girls in a new school funded by the government because it had 'come to the conclusion that it would be a good idea to educate the girls so that they could make suitable wives' for the new Nigerian professional men. The school was situated far out in the bush, near a town called Onitsha.

NOEL So I travelled out in 1929 – rather seasick – but full of hopes and ideas which suited me exactly. My first Sunday was a bit dramatic. We had to stay on the coast for the weekend because we didn't start travelling up land until the Monday. So I stayed with the couple who had the missionary bookshop in Port Harcourt. On Sunday morning, Tom, the husband, said to me, 'Well, I'm going to the lepers this morning. Would you like to come with me Noel?' Well, I was not that kind of person really, but I had to say, 'Yes, I'd love to go with you to the lepers.' So on Sunday morning I was plunged into a leper colony, with all these poor emaciated people gathered round. We had a service there.

That was the first Sunday morning. And then Sunday afternoon, his wife said to me, 'Oh, I'm going this afternoon to see all the poor women who are in prison – would you like to come with me?' Well of course I'd never been near a prison in my life! Oh the horror of going to a prison. And the poor women prisoners! Well that was my first Sunday! Life didn't go on quite like that, but I've never quite forgotten that.

Off we set the next day. It was the wet season and the roads were shocking. It was a remote place. And in Nigeria Europeans or foreigners couldn't ever own land. You had to hire it from the local tribes and all the land belonged to the chiefs. So we asked the chief for a bit of land to start this school, you see, and he gave us a hilltop out in the middle of nowhere, which seemed most attractive. It hadn't been farmed. Why? Because it was what you call ju-ju land – they used it for throwing away bad things. Ju-ju – you know, evil spirits. So nobody ever farmed there. Why? Because there were caves, and in these caves they had 'trial by ordeal'. A ju-ju or witch doctor lived there, and they used to send people through these caves. If you came out the other end alive, that meant that you'd won your case, the ju-ju had let you through. But if you didn't, the ju-ju had taken you off and blood would pour down the river. It wouldn't be the blood of the person, it would be the blood of a goat or something, and that person was really made into a slave and sold. For it was still in the days of slave trading, inland there. The idea was that those responsible for slavery were the white people, but it wasn't always. I only found that out after I'd been there for some time, but we didn't take any notice of it once we'd discovered about it. We didn't talk about it; no – it wasn't even mentioned.

We built a beautiful school there. We had six houses. They'd built a modern house for me a little way down the hill, of concrete blocks and a tin roof. I didn't have a mud house. It was supposed to be rather superior – but it was a bit lonely; in fact it was very lonely. Anyhow, there were lovely views, but we had primitive people all round us. For instance, this shows you how primitive it was. There was a deep valley in front of my house and then a hill up the other side and a village on the top of the hill. I used to hear all sorts of beautiful music coming from the village – dancing, moonlit nights and – oh, it was fascinating. But one time there was a lot of shouting and chaos, and we wondered why. Later we heard from a European policeman, who was a friend of ours, that some men in the village had killed a man coming from another village and eaten him. They were going to be had up and all the village was shouting about this.

So these men were taken to the town and were tried for murder. The four men all said, 'Ooh I didn't kill him. No, I didn't kill him.' 'But you ate him?' 'Oh yes, I ate him.' 'Why did you eat him?' 'Oh I wanted his "chee".' Now 'chee' was a man's spirit and the dead man had been a very powerful spirit in this other town. So they thought if they ate him they'd get his spirit inside them – his chee; they'd get his power and they'd be able to carry out all his witch doctoring, trials, and cures. So the court couldn't prove them of killing the man, so they got off scot-free. They were going to be hung in the village square to teach people not to eat each other, but they came back hale and hearty, frightfully pleased with themselves, and sat down in the square and had a wonderful beano with palm wine. They all got thoroughly drunk, rejoicing 'cos these men hadn't been hung. Well that was actually while I was there in the thirties, so it was pretty primitive.

So we had something to stand up to. There was an awful feeling of evil and we had to stand up to this sense of evil, which the girls had been brought up amongst. We just had to quietly go on, trying to live a Christian life and gradually we thought it would influence them. We didn't go out just with a Bible under our arm to preach the gospel. It wasn't like that at all.

The headmistress thought it was rather grand to introduce Scottish dancing to do at, I think, Empire Day – it sounds ridiculous. But they did literally learn, because they were very musical and they could pick up things like that. But it was all against my ideals to teach them Scottish dancing.

My headmistress was one of the old-school missionaries. She'd gone out untrained with all these good ideas about saving lost babies and things, but she wasn't a qualified teacher. We, well we, the qualified ones, had quite different ideas about education. So we were rather horrified to find that she and all the old teachers would go round the place with a stick in their hand and if somebody misbehaved they could just swipe with a stick, tell them they were being naughty or doing something wrong. Well of course that was not quite what we were expecting our education to be like, so it was a bit horrific at first. But after a year or two she went home on leave and I was fortunate enough to be left in charge.

Then it was very exciting. I got rid of all the sticks, I forbade the teachers ever to use a stick, and they were all burnt and thrown away. But then you had to put something in their place, if you were going to take all that kind of discipline away. For they were very naughty girls, strong and wilful, and they weren't easy to teach, not at all, and they had been brought up in heathen homes.

Anyhow, we just had to think of something else instead of all this corporal punishment. So we went round and we judged them for good marks. Instead of spending the first half an hour of the day scrubbing and doing all sorts of chores and then giving bad marks, we had the first quarter of an hour in silence in the chapel while the sun was rising – it was quite the most moving time. They could come if they liked or not. So the whole day started in a quiet way. Then we'd rush round and tidy up, have breakfast at seven and then we'd go round and

Above: At fifteen, Noel was sent to Wycombe Abbey school where she excelled in botany and music.
Top: Today she lives in an old Cotswold cottage near Amberley where she was born.

give them good marks. And we'd have competitions, who could make the best garden outside their house, to give them positive things to do. We also had competitions of native music and dancing and games, and give them marks for the best one and so on. And we began to collect all sorts of lovely native music.

We would suggest to them that they wrote their own Christmas carols. It was ridiculous to sing 'In the deep midwinter frosty wind did blow' and things like that. All our carols are wrapped up with winter and snow, and of course there's no such thing out there and they didn't know what it was all about. So I suggested that they should write their own lyrics and music, and we went out to the village churches and did lovely Nativity plays with all local music. That was so exciting, something really positive; and they all got good marks for things like that.

The government didn't give any grants for anything religious so we built our own chapel. It was really a tremendous event in their lives. Instead of being rather haughty, proud, superior students of education, they would have to put on their dirty old clothes and they made the bricks and gave them to the men who were building the chapel. We had a thatched roof of course, an absolutely traditional design. It fell down once in a storm but we built it up again, and that's where I was married.

I don't remember much about my wedding day, it's sort of blank to me. We walked from my house down to this chapel – and quite unknown to me the Chiefs had all turned up and they were wearing all their wonderful robes, gorgeous colours, oranges and reds, and wonderful hats, all at the back of our little mud chapel. All the rest were Europeans. The bishop married us. We signed the register and we got out into the open, and then all the college girls were round us and they danced traditional wedding songs and dances and they followed us all the way back up, dancing and clapping. And then – I feel ashamed nowadays, it seems funny doesn't it? – we had a wedding party up in my house, for all the Europeans, but there weren't any Africans there. Harold and I thought that what they would like would be a goat, a whole goat, and endless amounts of rice – which we had provided the money for – down in the college hall. We went down and talked to them, but that was what you'd call apartheid really, but I didn't feel it was funny then. But looking back on it, I feel almost ashamed. We wouldn't do that now, but that was what it was like.

Then we dressed and went off on the railway, and got on this funny little chug-chug boat in Port Harcourt, and sailed down the creeks to where Harold's District Office was. When we got there it was pitch dark, but all his staff and people had come out to meet us and the whole place was lit up with little twinkling bush lamps – and the river sort of twinkled with them. Oh, it was a wonderful moment.

Noel and her husband returned to England before the Second World War and she continued teaching until her retirement, with some further spells living abroad, including some time in Cyprus. They had three children. Now a widow, she lives on her own in a picturesque Cotswold cottage with a fine garden, next door to her daughter. Noel plays in a local string quartet, and on Sundays walks across the fields to the church, to join the service and the singing.

Julius Summerhayes, the 'baby' of the family, born in 1906, qualified as a doctor and, following in his sister Mary's footsteps, went to Uganda to work as a junior doctor in the hospital at Kampala.

JULIUS The missionary doctors I met at school – on leave, and as fathers of my friends – gave me an extra interest in medical missionary work. I was keen to be a doctor anyway, and growing up in an atmosphere of missionary work and Christian work sort of pointed to medical missions abroad.

Julius at the age of six – 'a sweet little boy'.

When I first got there, of course it wasn't long since the days of persecution and horrors. There was a lot of massacres of young boys and all that sort of thing for following the Christian faith, and so the Christian faith was still young and very much alive and they, the Africans, took to it in a big way.

It was a happy country and a happy people, which put us to shame in some ways. One little illustration of their sort of attitude to life: I sometimes had to drive a sort of hospital ambulance through the grassy tracks, as there weren't very many tarred roads, with high elephant grass on both sides. The local Africans usually got about on bicycles, wearing their long white robes like the old Roman toga. You'd come up behind an African pedalling along and as there was no room for both of us he used to head off into the elephant grass and fall off his bicycle. You'd sort of expect this howl, but instead there were roars of laughter. It was all a great joke, and life was very cheery with them.

I had the feeling that with a medical training you had something to give and you may as well give it where it was rather particularly needed. In Uganda there was plenty of work – a lot of illness, the birth mortality rate was very high and all sorts of tropical diseases added to all our ordinary medical troubles. One had plenty of opportunity for service.

That 'opportunity for service' took Julius to the primitive bush country in the southern Sudan to help a dying Scottish doctor run a leper colony.

My neighbouring doctor was two hundred miles away. And leprosy then had no cure. Once a week there was a clinic to which they came and would say to me, 'I want this off, or that off.' You know, it was rotted and getting in the way and troublesome. But the nerves were dead and you could amputate bits of limbs without any anaesthetic at all. But I remember, going to bed, one could always hear them singing hymns at night. They were happy.

Julius returned from Africa and practised as a GP in Deal until his retirement. He married and had four children, all of whom have pursued medical careers. Very recently widowed, he lives near the sea in Walmer, Kent, where he is one of the judges at the local flower show and is active in his local church.

The only mild dissenter in the Summerhayes family was the fourth child, Eirene, the 'piggy in the middle', who was born in 1898. She considered herself as 'a bit of a rebel' because unlike her siblings she did not want to become a missionary or work abroad. She was very keen on sport and after playing hockey for an English team in the United States, she returned home to become a housemistress at Benenden, the girls' public school, where she introduced the game of lacrosse.

As a married woman settled in England, she became the one who looked after her brothers' and sisters' children in the absence of their parents abroad.

EIRENE I was at school when the First World War began, and then mother said she thought it was time I came home from school and did some war work. She had heard about a convalescent home down in Weston-super-Mare and it would be a good idea for me to go there and be a nurse. Well, I knew nothing about nursing. But I went and we lived in a nurses' house which opened out onto the beach. We got into terrible trouble because we used to go out onto the beach in the evenings. Oh it was shocking! I'd meet some men!

The hospital was at the far end of the Esplanade, and it got overrun with rats. One day I went down to the kitchen to get some more jam or something, and there was a rat sitting on the end of a pot, dipping its tail into it! Eventually it was closed, but the matron kept on one or two of us, really, as her maids. And in the end I was left alone with her. I used to have to sleep in her room and I did dislike it. We had nobody in the hospital. Fortunately, Christopher, who was in the army, came home on leave and mother wrote to matron to ask if she would let me have some time off to see him. I packed my trunk and I took it with me,

and I said to mother, 'I'm not going back.' And when she heard, mother said, 'No dear, I had no idea!' Oh, it was so bad.

I didn't want to go out of England. I thought, I don't want to be a missionary (they were all so pious); I should be no good. So I said, 'I'm not going abroad.' 'Well,' they said, 'you'll have to look after our children.' So I had them live with me. I only had one [son] so there was plenty of room. I used to have a house crammed-jammed with children.

I thought I was, you know, not as good as they were – and I didn't think that I'd be any good as a missionary, and I was going to stay in England. One by one they went off and I admired them

Eirene knew 'nothing about nursing' but excelled at sports. 'I was a bit of a rebel'.

as they were all very splendid, but they were much better than I was – I had the sort of feeling that I wasn't sufficiently good. Oh yes! I was the heathen.

We were always brought up with the idea that we must serve the people we lived amongst. And I saw no reason why one couldn't do that in England.

Eirene has recently moved from her family home in Limpsfield, Surrey, to a warden-assisted apartment which was chosen for her by her husband before he died. Her son lives nearby, in the same village where the ex-missionary school, St Michael's, is situated. Until recently, she was playing a weekly round of golf.

Of the seven Summerhayes children, only the older boy, Christopher, was not alive to contribute to this remarkable family testimony of service to others: he died in 1988 leaving a widow and four children. Christopher had become a diplomat and was knighted for his services abroad; after fighting and being wounded in the First World War, he had gone on to become the British Ambassador to Nepal.

But was it their faith, the influence of their parents, or the desire to escape the strictures of Edwardian society that made this remarkable family so willing to serve others?

MARY We all grew up with the feeling that that was what you did – you went abroad. It was very much the days of the British Empire, but we were all, in our generation and further back, teachers and doctors, and the way to teach was to go through missionary schools and go to Africa. We were brought up on Livingstone and the Slave Trade and those heroic days. It seemed the natural thing to do. I didn't think of staying in England really. I was always half homesick for England when I was abroad, but still that's a different matter.

Grace with her student nurses in Ghana, 1929

NOEL The thirties were a wonderful period. It was just the right time to go out and be venturesome and do things. God, I think, used our parents and He used all sorts of other things. But I do feel very strongly that we all wanted to do something interesting and useful, whether it was my eldest brother who was a diplomat, my youngest brother who was a doctor, Mary a bishop's wife – and Grace a doctor, Mercy and Eirene teachers and so on. We've been very, very fortunate, I think.

Afterword: Listening to Living Memory

Many of you, reading or seeing *The Nineties,* will think of other older people you know who also have fascinating memories of their lives. Some will be members of your own family, others living in your community; and although some will also be in their nineties, others will be in their seventies or eighties. Is it worthwhile to record some of their memories too?

The answer is almost certainly 'yes': provided you do the job skilfully, recording the sound well and asking questions sensitively. How do you find out about this? The best introductory book is Paul Thompson, *The Voice of the Past* (Oxford paperback, 1988); you can read the brief pamphlet by Robert Perks, *Oral History* (Historical Association, 1992); and ask your local library for the journal *Oral History* (published by the Oral History Society, University of Essex, Colchester C04 3SQ).

If you have recorded a particularly interesting life story, you should consider offering it to a public archive. There is a network of local sound archives for tapes in libraries and record offices throughout the country. Copies of the tapes recorded for *The Nineties,* including many more than those used in the book or the broadcasts, have been deposited with the National Life Story Collection at the National Sound Archive, which now has an important oral history section. For advice on the archive or more generally on oral history, you can write to the Curator in Oral History, Robert Perks, National Sound Archive, Exhibition Road, London SW7 2AS.